AF279403

THE SOURCE OF SUPREME BLISS

THE DECHEN LING PRACTICE SERIES

THE SOURCE OF SUPREME BLISS

Heruka Chakrasamvara Five Deity Practice and Commentary

Ngulchu Dharmabhadra and
the First Panchen Lama,
Losang Chökyi Gyaltsen

Translated by David Gonsalez

Wisdom

Wisdom Publications
199 Elm Street
Somerville, MA 02144 USA
wisdomexperience.org

Library of Congress Cataloging-in-Publication Data
Names: Dngul-chu Dharmabhadra, 1772–1851, author. | Gonsalez, David, 1964–2014, translator. |
    Blo-bzang-chos-kyi-rgyal-mtshan, Panchen Lama I, 1570–1662.
    Grub-pa'i-dbaṅ-phyug Dril-bu-źabs lugs kyi zab lam rim lṅa'i dmar khrid śin tu zab pa. English.
Title: Source of supreme bliss: Heruka Chakrasamvara five deity practice and commentary /
    Ngulchu Dharmabhadra and the First Panchen Lama, Losang Chökyi Gyaltsen; translated by
    David Gonsalez.
Description: First wisdom edition. | Somerville: Wisdom Publications, 2022. |
    Series: Dechen ling practice series | Includes index.
Identifiers: LCCN 2021049415 (print) | LCCN 2021049416 (ebook) |
    ISBN 9781614295679 (hardcover) | ISBN 9781614295921 (ebook)
Subjects: LCSH: Tripiṭaka. Sūtrapiṭaka. Tantra. Cakrasamvaratantra—Criticism, interpretation, etc.
Classification: LCC BQ2180.C357 D68 2022 (print) | LCC BQ2180.C357 (ebook) |
    DDC 294.3/82—dc23/eng/20220517
LC record available at https://lccn.loc.gov/2021049415
LC ebook record available at https://lccn.loc.gov/2021049416

ISBN 978-1-61429-567-9 ebook ISBN 978-1-61429-592-1
25 24 23 22 22   5 4 3 2 1

Cover and interior design by Gopa & Ted2, Inc.

The drawing of twelve-armed Chakrasamvara on page iv by Robert Beer.
The line drawings on pages 2 and 118 and the color image of Chakrasamvara are © 2022 Andy Weber.

Printed on acid-free paper that meets the guidelines for permanence and durability of the Production Guidelines for Book Longevity of the Council on Library Resources.

Printed in the United States of America.

Contents

Publisher's Note to the New Edition

It is a pleasure for Wisdom Publications to bring out the *Dechen Ling Practice Series*. Ven. Losang Tsering provided a great kindness to qualified practitioners when he made available in English these incredible texts, which combine the depth of Madhyamaka philosophy with the sophistication of Vajrayana practices, as found in Lama Tsongkhapa's rich tradition.

Some time ago, I expressed to Ven. Losang Tsering that these texts had been helpful in my own practice, and this led to conversations about Dechen Ling Press collaborating with Wisdom Publications. Not long before Ven. Losang Tsering passed, we both agreed that Wisdom Publications would be an excellent place to preserve the legacy of these books and make them available to practitioners throughout the world. I am very happy to see the fruition of our intentions. May this series be a support for practitioners under the guidance of qualified teachers.

Daniel Aitken

Preface

THIS BOOK consists of a series of texts on the tantric teachings of Chakrasamvara that have been translated over the course of many years. This is not a scholarly work but one intended for practitioners. For that reason, annotations, notes, and so forth, have been kept to a minimum. The practice of Chakrasamvara should be done under the guidance of a qualified lama; therefore you should seek clarifications from him or her. The book begins with biographies of two important lamas of the Gelug tradition, Ngulchu Dharmabhadra and Yangchen Drupay Dorje. The main text in this book is a commentary on the five deity generation-stage practice of Heruka Chakrasamvara. This was an oral commentary given by Ngulchu Dharmabhadra in the nineteenth century, and the notes from this teaching were compiled by Yangchen Drupay Dorje into the text translated here. It is for this reason that I requested my lama, Gen Lobsang Choephel, to compose these two short biographies to serve as an introduction to the lives of these two illustrious lamas.

The next text is a highly restricted and secret text on the completion stage of Chakrasamvara in the tradition of Ghantapa, composed by the First Panchen Lama Losang Chökyi Gyaltsen. This is the first time that any portion of this text has been translated into English. Next in the collection is Ngulchu Dharmabhadra's retreat instruction. While certain sections of this text have already been covered in the main commentary, this text provides essential instructions on the rituals necessary for completing a proper retreat on Chakrasamvara five deity.

Part 2 is a collection of the relevant ritual texts. These will not only prove helpful for those wishing to engage in the practice but will also serve as a reference for following the commentary.

Of course, over the years of working on this material, I have received a great deal of assistance in rendering the book that you have in your hands now. I would like to express my gratitude to my former language teacher, Lobsang Thonden, who has been tireless in his dedication to helping me get this material properly translated. I met with him on a regular basis to help with difficult passages and clarify some of the intended meanings. Without his help it would have been very difficult to complete the translation of these texts.

I would like to thank Sidney Piburn of Snow Lion Publications for his long-term commitment to bringing this project to completion and his constant support and encouragement. My gratitude as well to my editor at Snow Lion, Michael Wakoff.

I would also like to thank Keith Milton, James Groshon, Karolyn McKinley, and Wolfgang Saumweber for their various contributions.

Most of all I would like to thank all of my lamas who have guided me throughout the years and, in particular, Gen Lobsang Choephel, who bestowed numerous empowerments, transmissions, and commentaries throughout our long relationship and who is an extraordinary practitioner and scholar.

I would also like to thank Susan and David Heckerman for their continued support throughout the years, which affords me the opportunity to spend all my time translating, studying, and engaging in retreats, and for supporting various projects that I have been involved with throughout the years.

The section concerning the measurements of the celestial mansion was translated by Alex Berzin.

The line drawings on pages 2 and 116 and the color image of Chakrasamvara were graciously provided by Andy Weber. His artwork is available in fine art prints at his website at www.andyweberstudios.com.

The three-dimensional mandala in the insert is from my private collection, and the photographs were taken by Joel Fraser.

David Gonsalez

A Brief Biography of Ngulchu Dharmabhadra

Ngulchu Dharmabhadra was born in the upper region of Tsang Yä Rü'i Cha in the region of Rong Tö Chug Mo, in the third *rab-jung* of the Water Dragon Year (1772). His father was Tashi Päljor and his mother Kadro Pälkyi.

When he was eleven years old, he learned the alphabet from his elderly uncle. From then on, whenever he met someone learned, he would seize the opportunity to study the alphabet with them. As he spent most of his time tending sheep, whenever he found a flat, smooth rock or level ground, he would practice his writing using only his fingers, which would often cause them to bleed. However, this didn't discourage him. Instead, he carried on until after a short time he learned all of the letters of *uchen* and *uchung*,[1] thus becoming an expert at reading and writing. Later on, the Venerable One was to become a holder of the treasury of secrets of all the conquerors. According to many scholars and pandits, it was clear that he was endowed with the characteristics of Vajradhara abiding in human form. In this regard, as it says in the twenty-fifth chapter of the *Key to the Secret Prophecies of the Great Knowledge Holder Padmasambhava*,

> In a place called Je and Podong,
> Will come one with the name of Dharmabhadra,
> An emanation of Vajradhara
> Who will turn the wheel of secret mantra teachings.
> Whoever has a connection with this one

---

1. *Uchen* and *uchung* are two forms of Tibetan script. The latter is equivalent to *ume*, or cursive script.

Ngulchu Dharmabhadra

Will reach the state of irreversibility
After seven rebirths.

This one of noble family with the name of Dharma
Was born in the area of Tsang.
Whoever at the time of death,
When all appearance of this life sets,
Should hear the name of this one,
Will attain the state of perfect joy.

Also,

Between Eh and Dar an emanation of Vajrapani will arise
Whose name will be Dharmabhadra.

These verses clearly show Ngulchu's name and designate his birthplace as being between Podong Eh and Je Dar Ting. When he was still very young, whenever monks came to visit his family, they were all so surprised by his manner of thinking and acting and by his exceptional skill at reading and writing that they could not believe he was an ordinary person. Accordingly, they were all convinced that if he were to apply himself to Dharma, he would certainly become an excellent student.

At the age of fourteen, he was admitted to Tashi Gephel Monastery. It was there that he was given the name of Losang Tsering by Master Losang Gyaltsen. Early on, since he was skilled at writing, he was given one page of Ganden Lha Gyama, handwritten by Khedrup Ngawang Dorje, and was told to copy it.[2] By the sheer act of copying the text, he memorized it, and just by seeing Khedrup Ngawang Dorje's handwriting, he developed great faith and requested an audience with him. Due to his great faith, the moment he met [Khedrup Ngawang Dorje], all impure appearances immediately disappeared, and he began to weep profusely. It was from this that Khedrup Ngawang Dorje recognized that Ngulchu was a special being, and so from then on, he gave him very meaningful, heartfelt advice,

---

2. Ganden Lha Gyama (Tib. *dga' ldan lha brgya ma*) is a guru yoga practice of Lama Tsongkhapa, which is translated as "One Hundred Deities of Tushita."

and with great love he gave him copious instruction on both the sutras and tantras, like filling one vase from another. In return, [Ngulchu] protected these instructions as if they were his own eyes. He received the novice vows of individual liberation directly from the great Khedrup and was given the name Wangchuk Chösang.

From the age of eighteen to nineteen, [Ngulchu] experienced a very sad period in his life when three people very close to him—his elder brother Tadrin Wangyel, his mother, and his aunt—died, one after the other. As a result, with the permission of his lama, he went into retreat in an isolated place to practice single-pointedly, where he remained until he was twenty. After this time, he was admitted into the ranks of a *gelong*[3] and went to Ngulchu Cave, where he listened and contemplated with great effort. In the tenth month of that same year, he received the complete training as a gelong from Lopön Yeshe Päldrup, and consequently he had a lot to learn, such as how to obtain water, how to bless one's belongings, how to give and receive various small articles, and so forth. As a gelong he practiced perfectly, maintaining complete moral discipline, and so he became a great Vinaya holder.[4] From the age of twenty-two to thirty-two, he returned again and again to Tashi Lhunpo,[5] meanwhile studying with such masters as Drongtse Losang Tsultrim and Yongzin Gugay Losang Tenzin, to name a few. In this way he studied with many learned pandits and listened to many teachings on both the common teachings and the uncommon teachings of sutra and tantra.

From the age of thirty-five on, he mainly practiced meditation but also taught extensively on the three important subjects of exposition, debate, and composition. At this time he also composed various works on sutra and tantra, which constitute six volumes of teachings. He had many disciples, such as Yangchen Drupay Dorje, Khenchen Ngawang Nyendrak, Ripuk Tulku Losäl Tenkyong, and Dechen Tulku Losang Tsultrim, among others.

At the age of seventy, he made offerings to forty-one monasteries in

---

3. The Tibetan word *gelong* (Tib. *dge slong*) is a translation of the Sanskrit word *bhikshu*, which means a fully ordained monk.
4. The Vinaya is the set of teachings concerned with the moral discipline of monks and nuns.
5. Tashi Lhunpo is a famous monastery in Shigatse founded by the First Dalai Lama that was later to become the seat of the Panchen Lamas.

Shay. Throughout his life, up to the age of eighty, he traveled to Truzin to give teachings several times. However, he spent most of his time staying in Ngulchu Cave, where he engaged solely in meditation. When he was eighty, on the eighth day of the fourth month of the Iron Pig Year (1851), for the sake of those to be subdued, he passed away into the *dharmakaya*.

In a mahamudra commentary written by Gaden Kälsöl is a request to the [lineage lamas] that says,

> With the skill and stability of a second conqueror,
> The Protector who illuminated the Conqueror's teachings
> With clear exposition,
> To Jetsun Dharmabhadra, I make my request.

Colophon

Composed by Zephuk Gelong Lobsang Choephel.

A Brief Biography of Yangchen Drupay Dorje

A s FOR Yangchen Drupay Dorje Losang Chöphel's place of birth, from
among the three—U, Tsang, and Kham[6]—he was born in Tsang
near Tashi Gephel Ling. In earlier times, this place was called Je, but later,
since Padmasambhava had smiled three times when he visited it, the name
of the place was changed to Shay (meaning "smile") as a good omen.
Yangchen Drupay Dorje was born to Ngulchu Dharmabhadra's younger
brother Tashi and his wife Tsering Sichö, during the fourteenth rabjung in
the Earth Snake Year of 1809, on the evening of the fifth day of the tenth
month, among numerous wondrous signs.[7]

In 1813, at the age of five, he received the commentary on grammar
and the oral transmission of the *Situ* text from his uncle, the all-knowing
Dharmabhadra, and he began learning the alphabet. At that time his name
was Jamyang Dorje, and at only six years of age, he had engaged in extensive studies with various lamas and excelled in learning and memoriza-
tion, completing everything without obstruction.

In 1818, in his tenth year, near the cave of Lama Losang, in another cave
called Gyamo Trapuk, there was a lama named Tobgyel Lama Ngawang
Nyendrak, from whom Yangchen Drupay Dorje received many teachings. All the favorable conditions for living were given to him by Kuwo
Chösang. There he studied astrology and charts, thus memorizing all
the descriptions of everything [necessary for astrology]. At that time his

---

6. U is in the center of Tibet, Kham to the east, and Tsang to the west.
7. A rabjung is a sixty-year cycle. Thus the fourteenth rabjung is 840 years since the establish-
ment of the current system of the Tibetan calendar. Thanks to Glenn Mullin for this information.

maternal grandmother, who had a great deal of affection for him, passed away. Therefore, when his grandmother passed away, he went home for a short while.

When he returned again, he began listening and contemplating with great enthusiasm. In 1819, at the age of eleven, when all the monks related to Tashi Gephel Monastery had assembled, he was accepted into the monastery. Gachen Könchok Chöphel performed the hair-cutting ceremony, and he received the name Losang Chöphel.

In 1820, at the age of twelve, in the Iron Dragon Year, he received the layperson's vows and the novice monk's vows from Gachen Könchok Chöphel. At that point he began reading Milarepa's biography, his spiritual songs, and so forth. In this way he studied many texts. When he read the *Hundred Thousand Songs of Milarepa*, his faith and pure view were greatly increased.

In 1827, at the age of nineteen, Lama Chösang accepted him as his disciple. Beginning with language, astrology, poetry, grammar, and so forth, he then began listening, contemplating, and meditating on the great texts of sutra and tantra. He also trained in measurements of sand and three-dimensional mandalas and so forth, studying them extensively.

In 1842, at the age of thirty-four, in the Water Tiger Year, he studied poems and the Kalapa language[8] with his lama and passed the exams perfectly, thus pleasing his lama, who said to him, "You did excellently." He presented him with a long khata and then gave him the name of Yang-chen Drupay Dorje.[9] From that point on, his name gained great renown, and his fame spread.

At the age of thirty-four, on the fifteenth day of the fourth month, he received the vows of a gelong. He received the commentary on the gelong vows and the cycle of profound teachings on the Vinaya and, like a vast ocean, he trained purely in the moral discipline. Next, he gradually received all the profound teachings from his lama, like one vase filling another, and eventually he received them all. He then compiled all the teachings of his lama [Ngulchu Dharmabhadra] and composed works on some of

8. This is a form of Sanskrit.
9. The Tibetan word "Yangchen" is a translation of "Sarasvati," the name of the goddess of poetry and language. Thus his guru named him "Accomplished One—Sarasvati Vajra," an extremely flattering way of expressing his accomplishment in language and poetry.

them. In between he did the retreat of the supreme deity and fulfilled the needs of many people by giving empowerments and commentaries.

In 1851, at the age of forty-three, during the fourteenth rabjung in the Iron Pig Year on the eighth day of the fourth month, his kind lama [Ngul-chu Dharmabhadra] dissolved his appearance back into the dharmakaya. Up to this point he had lived with his lama for twenty-four years without being separated from him, and thus he was quite upset at the loss of his lama. Therefore, he built a reliquary for his lama's remains and built a silver stupa, and thus perfectly completed his [lama's] wishes.

From this point on he upheld the responsibility of being a lama throughout the monastery, building new statues as well as giving extensive teachings. Not only that, but he also published his lama's complete teachings and made corrections to them.

In 1869, at the age of sixty-one, in the fifteenth rabjung of the Earth Dragon Year, he traveled to Sakya, Tashi Lhunpo, and Lhasa. In central Tibet he made prostrations and offerings to all of the sacred objects. He gave advice to all the great lamas of the three monasteries as well as one of the cabinet members. Again and again he gave the nectar of the Dharma to them all.

After more than one year in central Tibet, in 1870, in the Earth Horse Year, in his sixty-second year, he returned to the great monasteries and once again gave teachings. He raised high the victory banner of the Gelugpa lineage of teaching and practice. All the great scholars of the Land of Snow held him as their crown ornament.

In 1887, at the age of seventy-six, in the fifteenth rabjung of the Fire Pig Year, on the sixteenth day of the tenth month, as he passed away, he showed the complete aspect of being a holy being. Spending his entire life working for the Dharma, his life is without comparison.

He had many disciples including Drakchen Ngawang Tsultrim, Gongma Lharampa Gendun Gyatso, Lama Yeshe Chöphel, Mindröl Nominhan, Chabdo Phakpa Lha, Chusang Hutoktu, Laylungma Lama Tsultrim Gyelsten, Losang Jikme, and so forth.

The compilation of his collected works contains seventy-seven texts and constitutes three volumes.

As written in the request to the mahamudra lineage lamas of the Ganden oral lineage,

Your great eyes of unobservable compassion never close.
Your vast and profound wisdom is like that of Manjushri.
To Yangchen Drupay Dorje I make request.

Colophon

Composed by Zephuk Gelong Lobsang Choephel.

PART 1

Commentaries

Ngulchu Dharmabhadra's
Heruka Five Deity Commentary

Outline

How to Practice during the Actual Session
How to Practice during the Meditation Break

The first has three parts:
1. How to Begin the Session
2. How to Engage in the Actual Session
3. How to End the Session

How to Begin the Session has two parts:
1. Engaging in the Preliminary Stage
2. How to Accomplish the Branches of Yoga

Engaging in the Preliminary Stage has five parts:
1. Arranging the Various Articles of Yoga
2. Going for Refuge and Generating Bodhichitta
3. Instantaneous Self-Generation
4. Blessing the Inner Offering
5. Blessing the [Outer] Offerings

Arranging the Various Articles of Yoga has two parts:
1. Motivation
2. Requesting the Lineage Gurus

Going for Refuge and Generating Bodhichitta has two parts:
1. Going for Refuge
2. Generating Bodhichitta

Going for Refuge has four parts:
1. Visualizing the Object of Refuge
2. Establishing the Cause of Going for Refuge
3. The Actual Act of Going for Refuge
4. The Descent of Purifying Nectar

Generating Bodhichitta
Instantaneous Self-Generation
Blessing the Inner Offering
Blessing the Outer Offerings has four parts:
1. Cleansing [the Outer Offerings]
2. Purifying [the Outer Offerings]
3. Generating [the Substances of the Outer Offerings]
4. Blessing [the Outer Offerings]

How to Accomplish the Branches of Yoga has four parts:
1. Accumulating the Collection of Merit
2. Bringing Death into the Path of the Truth Body
3. Bringing the Intermediate State into the Path of the Enjoyment Body
4. Meditating on the Protection Circle

Accumulating the Collection of Merit has three parts:
1. Invoking the Field of Merit
2. Collecting the Accumulation of Merit has three parts:
    1. Prostration
    2. Making Outer, [Inner, Secret, and Suchness] Offerings
    3. Confessing and Rejoicing
3. Dissolving the Field of Merit

Bringing Death into the Path of the Truth Body
Bringing the Intermediate State into the Path of the Enjoyment Body
Meditating on the Protection Circle
How to Engage in the Actual Session has seven parts:
1. Generating the Seat for the Celestial Mansion

2. Generating the Supporting and Supported Mandalas by Taking Rebirth into the Path of the Emanation Body
3. Generating the Third "Manifest Enlightenment"
4. Generating the Fourth "Manifest Enlightenment"
5. Generating the Fifth "Manifest Enlightenment"
6. Visualizing the Stages of That Generation
7. Visualizing the Supporting Celestial Mansion

Visualizing the Supported Deities has two parts:
1. Visualizing the Principal [Deity]
2. Visualizing the Retinue

Visualizing the Principal [Deity] has two parts:
1. Visualizing the Principal Father
2. Visualizing the Principal Mother

Visualizing the Retinue has two parts:
1. Visualizing the Four Goddesses in the Directions
2. Visualizing the Vases and Skull Cups in the Intermediate Directions

Meditating on the Corresponding Purity has three parts:
1. Blessing the Four Places
2. From Blessing the Secret Place to Inducing the Four Joys
3. The Actual Meditation on the Purity

Wearing the Armor and the Entering of the Wisdom Beings has two parts:
1. Wearing the Armor
2. Entering of the Wisdom Beings

From Bestowing Empowerment up to the Sealing has two parts:
1. Bestowing Empowerment
2. Sealing with the Lord of the Lineage

From Making Offerings and Praises up to Meditating
on the Mandala has three parts:
    1. Making Offerings
    2. Making Praises
    3. Meditating on the Mandala

Making Offerings has five parts:
    1. Making Outer Offerings
    2. Inner Offering
    3. The Secret and Suchness Offerings
    4. Offering the Mantras
    5. Offering Praise

Meditating on the Mandala
How to End the Session has four parts:
    1. How to Engage in the Recitation
    2. How to Offer the Tormas
    3. How to Withdraw [the Visualization]
    4. How to Make the Dedication Prayers

How to Engage in the Recitation has four parts:
    1. Blessing the Rosary for Recitation
    2. Visualization [during] the Recitation
    3. How to Engage in the Recitation
    4. Ending the Recitation

How to Offer the Tormas
How to Withdraw [the Visualization]
How to Make the Dedication Prayers
How to Practice during the Meditation Break
The Benefits of Such a Meditation
Colophon
Second Colophon
Translator's Colophon

NOTES ON THE GENERATION STAGE OF HERUKA FIVE
DEITIES IN THE TRADITION OF MAHASIDDHA GHANTAPA,
ENTITLED *THE ESSENCE OF GREAT BLISS*

NAMA SHRI CHAKRASAMVARAYA

WITH GREAT respect I prostrate and go for refuge at the feet of
the supreme guide Dharmabhadra, the venerable guru endowed
with great, unobservable compassion, who is inseparable from glorious
Heruka. I request that you please take care of us with your great compassion throughout all our lives.

> Vajradhara, the lord of the lineage of an ocean of conquerors,
> Through the display of your unobservable compassion,
>   you manifest as
> The spiritual friend for the sake of those to be subdued;
> I bow to Dharmabhadra endowed with the three types
>   of kindness.

> Perfectly embraced by the vermillion-colored joyous Mother,
> Glorious Heruka, the lord of all things stable and moving,
> Together with the four goddesses of great bliss,
> May the lords of the mandala protect me.

Introduction

As is said as well by Master Shantideva,

> This [body] of leisure and endowments is so difficult to find,
> That once attained can accomplish the welfare of living beings;

> If you don't accomplish its benefit now,
> It will be very difficult to get this opportunity again.

Now we have obtained this human body of leisure and endowments that is so difficult to find, and we have met the sacred Dharma, which is so hard to meet. At this time when we have the ability and intelligence to discern, without error, which actions to adopt and which ones to abandon, if we are only concerned with finding food, clothing, and shelter until the time of our death, we will never be content. We must be able to identify methods for bringing benefit to our future lives in samsara. Furthermore, our teacher [Buddha Shakyamuni], who had great love for all beings without discrimination and was called "Guru Buddha Tathagata of the Three Worlds," whose fame has spread throughout all the three worlds, is one who observes perfectly the worlds, minds, and propensities of trainees and spontaneously turns the wheel of Dharma in accordance with their individual dispositions. Ultimately the various teachings are definitely included within the two vehicles—the Mahayana and the Hinayana. Within the Mahayana there are also definitely two vehicles: the tantric vehicle and the perfection vehicle.[10] Furthermore, between these two, the tantric vehicle is superior in that one meditates on a path that is concordant with the aspects of a buddha's resultant body, abode, enjoyments, and deeds, [known] as the "four complete purities." Whether or not these are present is what distinguishes [the perfection vehicle from the tantric vehicle]. Given that these [four complete purities] *are not* existent in the perfection vehicle, it is referred to as the "causal vehicle," and because they *are* existent in the secret mantra vehicle, this latter is known as the "resultant vehicle." This is how they are individually posited.

Furthermore, concerning the resultant secret mantra vajrayana, it is stated in the *Embracing* [*Tantra*],

> Laughing, looking,
> Holding hands, and embracing each other:
> These abide in the four tantras in the manner of a worm.[11]

---

10. "Perfection" refers to the Mahayana sutra practices that incorporate the six perfections.

11. This quote refers to the way in which a worm is born in wood and then consumes that very wood. In the same way, through these four ways of interacting with a god or goddess, one generates

Thus, the four tantras—action, performance, yoga, and highest yoga tantra—are divided into outer actions and inner deity yoga. Of these two, the outer-action [tantras] are mostly concerned with conduct.

Tantras that are taught primarily for trainees who imagine that they are exchanging glances with a meditated goddess and thereby bring the occurrence of bliss into the path are action tantras.

Tantras that are taught when both the outer actions and the inner deity yoga are practiced equally and that are primarily taught for trainees who imagine that they are exchanging smiles with a meditated goddess and thereby incorporate that occurrence of bliss into the path are performance tantras.

Tantras that are taught when, of the two, outer actions and inner deity yoga, inner deity yoga is primarily practiced and that are principally taught for trainees who imagine that they are holding hands with a meditated goddess and incorporate that occurrence of bliss into the path are yoga tantras.

[Highest yoga tantra is established] when, of the two, [outer actions and inner deity yoga,] one primarily practices deity yoga, and it is taught principally for trainees who take the occurrence of bliss from the joining of the two organs into the path. Since there are no other tantras superior or higher, this tantra is posited as "unsurpassed."

Furthermore, when a tantra explicitly teaches the method to attain the illusory body, it is classified as belonging to father tantra. It is the factor of method that gives rise to the illusory body, on the side of appearance. This is the uncommon cause of the form body, and since it is similar to the seed of the father, it is a father tantra.

When a tantra doesn't principally teach the method for attaining the illusory body but instead explicitly teaches the method to attain the exalted wisdom of clear light—established as one taste in ultimate reality—that tantra is classified as belonging to mother tantra. Since the factor of the exalted wisdom of clear light, on the side of emptiness, is the common cause of the form body and is similar to the seed of the mother, it is a mother tantra.

---

bliss through desire, and then through that very blissful consciousness realizing emptiness, one destroys the delusions that gave rise to the bliss in the first place.

There are 160 million mother tantras, and of these the one that has the greatest and swiftest blessing in this degenerate era is this very tantra of the glorious Heruka Chakrasamvara. Furthermore, our teacher Vajradhara, in order to subdue the gods Ishvara and Kalarati, manifested the supporting mandala of Heruka upon Mount Meru and taught the root tantra. There are three root tantras: the longest [root tantra] is three hundred thousand verses, the middling one is one hundred thousand verses, and the shortest is fifty-one chapters.

Manifestation of Heruka says,

> The essence of that tantra was condensed from the explanation
> Of the hundred thousand and three hundred thousand.[12]

The explanatory tantras (1) *Vajradaka*, (2) *All Conducts of the Dakinis*, the two, (3) *Source of the Vows of Heruka* and *Manifestation of Vajravarahi*, which are counted as one, and (4) *The Direct Expression of the Guru* make up the four explanatory tantras of Heruka. The (5) *Sambhuta Tantra*, for its part, is common to [both Heruka and] Hevajra, making five [in all].[13]

Mitub Dawa [says],

> The *Source of the Dakinis* and *All Conducts*,
> Likewise, the *Tantra of the Supreme Name of the Guru*
> And *The Embracing*, thus make four;
> These should be known as the explanatory tantras.

The root and explanatory [tantras] were taught to Vajravarahi and the Lord of Secrets [Vajrapani]. Later on they were passed on to Saraha and then to Protector Nagarjuna. From him they passed on to glorious Shawari Wangchuk, then to the great master of Odiyana Luipa, from him to his direct disciple, King Darikapa, and then to Master Ghantapa.[14]

---

12. These two longer tantras were condensed into the abbreviated Chakrasamvara root tantra comprising fifty-one chapters and seven hundred verses.
13. In Tibetan, the five explanatory tantras are (1) *rDo rje mkha 'gro*, (2) *rNal 'byor ma kun sbyod*, (3) *bDe mchog sdom 'byung* and *Phag mo mngon 'byung*, (4) *mNgon brjod bla ma*, and (5) *Sambhuta*.
14. Here follows the biography of Mahasiddha Ghantapa.

When the master Ghantapa was staying in eastern India he was born as the royal prince to the king of Nalanda. After his father died, the ministers and so forth wanted to appoint him as the regent to the king, [but] seeing the kingdom had no essence, he declined. Gradually he traveled to glorious Nalanda, and in the presence of the abbot Gyalway Lha Rabtu Sangpo, he took ordination and was given the name "Glorious Essence of Intelligence." Training in the sciences, he became completely skilled in the Three Baskets and all sciences, and [became] a pandit.[15] He defeated many long-haired non-Buddhists in debate and as the victor became the crown ornament of the Conqueror's teaching and a pandit whom others were powerless [to defeat]. When the Master defeated them all, he established the Buddhist teaching and became famed as "The Master Victorious over the Enemy."

At that time he met Lama [King] Darikapa, to whom he bowed respectfully and made offerings, and after the king accepted these offerings, [Ghantapa] listened to the teachings of the Three Baskets from him. After [Ghantapa] requested that he be taken under his care, he was bestowed empowerment into the mandala of glorious Chakrasamvara and received the complete instructions and follow-up instructions. From a voice in the sky, he then received a prophecy to go to an isolated place to accomplish the [teachings]. [It said,] "If you go to an isolated forest in Bengal to accomplish this [practice], after a short while, if you go to Odiyana, you will be cared for by a female pig herder." Having gone there he offered prostrations and supplications to all the pig herders he saw but none replied. Then he met an ugly, old female pig herder who was sometimes laughing and sometimes crying. First having prostrated to her and made an offering, he then asked her, "Why are you acting in this way?" And she replied, "Even though tantra is flourishing, there are very few practitioners."

Realizing she was a dakini, he touched the crown of his head to her feet and requested to be accepted as her follower. Then she directly displayed her body as the mandala of Chakrasamvara and bestowed empowerment and the oral instructions. Thereafter she instructed him to go to the south

---

15. There are three "baskets" or sets of discourses within the Buddha's teaching: (1) the set of moral discipline or Vinaya, (2) the set of discourses or Sutranta, and (3) the set of wisdom or Abhidharma.

[of India] to meditate. So, the Master gradually made his way to the south [of India] to a place called Odivisha, at which time he took up his abode in an isolated forest to accomplish the essence [of his practice].

And while he was staying there, it so happened that the king of that country was on summer holiday to relieve his sadness. He traveled to the forest where there were wild animals upon which he could practice his archery. When that king came across the Master, seeing how extremely emaciated he was and how his body had been tormented by sun and wind and that he had absolutely nothing to survive on, the king felt compassion for him and said, "You should come to the city, and I will give you food." At that point the Master had attained the third stage by training in the five stages [of completion-stage practice], and the time had come for him to rely on an action mudra [physical consort]. So, through his clairvoyance he could see the consort with whom he was to practice.[16]

Ghantapa replied,

> You should not despise those who have completely mastered
> wisdom.
> Just as one does not become attached to something as small as
> a tip of grass,
> I am not attached to things like wealth.
> Just as an elephant cannot be led by a fine lotus thread,
> So too the continuity of my practice cannot be interrupted by
> droplets of beer.
> Therefore, let your cheeks turn black.

When the king heard this, he became quite angry and said, "I will disgrace this man in the city," and thereby returned to the city and pronounced, "I will give a large reward to whoever can disgrace this forest-dwelling ascetic and bring him to the city."

At this time a prostitute who had a beautiful daughter of the lotus lineage promised, "I will disgrace this man." So the king gave the woman

---

16. The five completion stages are speech isolation, mind isolation, illusory body, clear light, and union. To attain the illusory body before death, one must rely upon a physical consort, otherwise known as an "action mudra." These five stages should not be confused with the five stages of the completion stage of Ghantapa.

whatever she needed and then sent her from the city. When this girl requested to serve the Master, he saw that she was a fortunate being and gave her permission to stay. Thus she became a vessel for the empowerments and all the commitments. By relying on this action mudra, Ghantapa reached the culmination of the five stages at the end of twelve years. Then by practicing the "all good" conduct, they stayed in Odivisha to subdue those people living there who desired the Vajrayana. The Master said, "In the future the unfortunate sentient beings will have the intention to invoke an emanation of Chenrezig." So he decided that in order to correct the minds of those faithless beings, he would go to the city, and thus he emanated a boy and a girl. Then the king ordered a beer seller, a woman, saying, "Today, bring that monk from the forest." All the people of the city gathered in front of the doors to the city. Along the path they had beer vessels lined up and they invited the Master [to drink]. The emanated boy came along his right side and the emanated girl along his left. The Master was drinking beer from a horn vessel and poured some for his consort, so that the both of them were drinking beer.

In this way he gradually arrived while drinking beer, and when they reached the city, the king, who was in the center of the entire city's population, told them to sing the verse that the Master had previously recited. Even though the king invited him earlier, Ghantapa had refused to come. So the king said, "Now the Master is drinking beer and has children! When he arrives I want everyone to laugh at him and clap their hands."

According to the Master's earlier intention [to subdue the unfortunate beings] and in order to show them his power, he threw the horn vessel into the ground, and it went seven levels beneath the earth from which a big spring emerged. Immediately the Master transformed into Heruka, the woman into Vajravarahi, the emanated boy into a vajra, and the girl into a bell. And so, as the simultaneously born Heruka [Father and Mother], they embraced and traveled into the sky. Upon seeing this, the king and the people requested forbearance from the Master. So the Master instructed them to pray to Chenrezig. All the people were saying NAMO LOKESHVARAYA[17] as a request, and from within the middle of the water a statue of Chenrezig arose. The water circumambulated it

---

17. NAMO LOKESHVARAYA means "I prostrate to Chenrezig."

seven times and then sunk back into the ground. These days that statue of Chenrezig has great blessings and provides protection for all sentient beings. So it was that all the people of Odivisha entered the Vajrayana and achieved many attainments:

> The vajra seat as well as the children
> Found attainments and
> Fulfilled the prophecy in Bengal;
> To the guru called Ghantapa I prostrate.[18]

In this way, with the intention of benefiting the future generations of disciples, the great mahasiddha composed the ritual for the body mandala empowerment, the great and small sadhanas of the body mandala, the sadhana of the outer mandala of the five deities, the three sadhanas of the generation stage, the five stages of completion stage, and the two sadhanas of the simultaneous Heruka[19] and so forth.

Rubelshab received the meaning of the tantra together with the oral instructions [from Ghantapa]. From him it went to Parwazin, which is the translation equivalent of Dzalandaripa. From him it was bestowed on Nagpopa. Next it was bestowed on Guhyapa, or as he is known in Tibetan, Drubchen Sawgway Pel ("The Glorious Great Accomplished Secret One"). Then it was bestowed on Mahasiddha Namgyal Shab. Then it was bestowed on excellent and supreme Tilopa. Then it was bestowed on Naropa. Next it was bestowed on the Nepali Pamtingpa brothers; the older Jikmey Drakpa and the younger Ngawang Drakpa. Then it was bestowed on Lokya Sherab Tseg. Then it was bestowed on Mal Lotsawa Lodrö Drak. Then it was bestowed on Sachen Kunga Nyingpo. Then it was bestowed on the elder Sönam Tsemo and the younger Drakpa Gyaltsen. Then it was bestowed on Sapan Kunga Gyaltsen. Then it was bestowed on Drogön Chögyal Phakpa. Then it was bestowed on Shangton Konchok Pel. Then it was bestowed on Nasa Dragpukpa Sönam Pel. Then it was bestowed on Palden Lama Dampa Sönam Gyaltsen. Then it was bestowed

---

18. Here the vajra seat refers to the consort, or action mudra, that acts as a seat for the vajra, or penis, of the master.

19. This last one is a simple aspect of Heruka with one face, two hands, a consort, and without a retinue. For a translation of the extensive body mandala sadhana, visit www.dechenling.org.

on Jetsun Losang Drakpa [Tsongkhapa]. Then it was bestowed on the older brother Khedrup Gelek Palsang and then to his younger brother Baso Chögyen. Then it was bestowed on Dharmavajra, or as he is known in Tibetan, Chökyi Dorje. Then it was bestowed on those known as the father and son of Ensa—the father Losang Döndrup and the son Sangye Yeshe. Then it was bestowed on Panchen Losang Chökyi Gyaltsen. Then it was bestowed on Dorje Zinpa Konchok Gyaltsen. Then it was bestowed on the tulku of Kyi Sho Tenzin Trinley. Then it was bestowed on Zim Shak Khenpo Losang Khetsun. Then it was bestowed on Je Ngawang Jampa. Then it was bestowed on those known as Yongzin father and son—the father Pandit Yeshe Gyaltsen and the son Gugay Losang Tenzin. Then it was bestowed on my kind root guru, the sovereign lord of the lineage and the ocean of mandalas Lord Jetsun Dharmabhadra Palsangpo. He received these very profound instructions of the hearing lineage and had many various ways of explaining these teachings. He was the manifestation of all the limitless array of buddhas appearing in the aspect of a saffron-robed monk. He gave these teachings according to the omniscient Panchen Losang Chökyi Gyaltsen's sadhana, entitled *The Source of Great Bliss*.

Also, as for the disciples of the place of teaching, the tantra *Samvarodaya*[20] states,

> Stable, subdued, and intelligent,
> Patient, honest, and unwavering,
> Having completely abandoned the ten nonvirtues,
> They view all living beings with love.
>
> They do not touch other's wealth;
> That is like blazing fire and poison.
> Instead they continuously make offerings to the guru,
> Delight in the view of sacred Dharma,
> And take joy in giving and so forth.
>
> They are praised as the best disciples who
> Wish to transcend the world;

---

20. Tib. *sdom 'byung*.

> To them you should reveal the
> Virtuous mandala.

As for these characteristics, they will not arise in oneself from the beginning but should be generated through properly training the mind in stages. Also in the beginning [train in] proper reliance upon a spiritual master, then in the great meaning of freedom and endowments, then in the difficulty of finding [them], how they will not last long, and how after death, without any control, you will wander in the lower realms and observe for a long time the various sufferings of the hells and so forth. This is training in the common path and the way to properly train your mind in renunciation. Also, when you initially enter the Vajrayana, your mind should be endowed with great compassion. Next, if one explains the profound path of highest mantra to disciples who are unsuitable vessels, these disciples will be ruined, and it is said that the path of realizations and attainments for both the master and the disciple will be set far out of reach.

From the tantra *Vajra Mala*,

> Just as the milk of a [snow] lion
> Cannot be placed in an earthen vessel,
> Just so the tantra of great yoga
> Should not be given to impure vessels.
>
> [If it is], that disciple will die in an instant,
> And this and future [lives] will be ruined.
> If one explains the oral instructions to non-[suitable] vessels,
> The master's attainments will degenerate.

Therefore, it is a sacred, essential oral instruction to train the mind in the common path when initially entering the mantra [path]. Then, when entering the [Vajrayana], one should receive the complete four empowerments in the presence of a vajra master endowed with all of the characteristics.

From the *Drop of Mahamudra*,

First when the disciple is
Bestowed the empowerment once,
At that time explain the great secret and
[They] will definitely become vessels.

Without the empowerment,
There will be no attainments,
Just as you can't get butter from squeezing sand.

Whoever, with the pride of knowing tantra,
Teaches without empowerment,
As soon as the master and disciple die,
Although they [may] have attainments, they will go to hell.[21]

Therefore, with every effort you should
Request empowerment from the guru.

In the limitless tantras and texts of the mahasiddhas, it is said that if you have not entered the mandala, you are not suitable for engaging in tantric practice. After receiving empowerment and training in the path, you must know perfectly the vows and commitments that you have promised [to maintain] at the time of the empowerment. Don't just leave them as mere promises, but cherish them at all times as you would your life, and make a great effort to protect whatever you know to the best of your ability, and be earnest in protecting them. Without [maintaining your vows], it is not suitable to [call yourself] a practitioner.

From the *Fifth Commitment*,

If you don't have a downfall,
There will be attainments in sixteen lifetimes.

---

21. Although it may be possible to accomplish some attainments from receiving an empowerment from one who does not have the empowerment, at the moment of death both the guru and disciple will go to hell as a result.

From the *Liberating Moon*,

> Even if you don't meditate but don't have a downfall,
> You will become realized in sixteen lifetimes.

Therefore, we must abide in the commitments purely and then begin meditating on the two stages. We must be thoroughly trained in the methods of meditating on the two stages together with their limbs through listening, contemplation, and wisdom. Otherwise, without any knowledge of the many ways in which we can go wrong with respect to how to practice, then no matter how much effort we put into our practice, either it will not bear fruit, or we may obtain a variety of undesired results and might end up just anywhere.

Concerning that, the Hevajra [text] entitled *A Pearl Rosary of Difficult Explanations* says,

> Without intelligence, without hearing, and not hearing as well as not contemplating; yoga separated from these two, and those separated from yoga—there will be no attainments.

From the *Five Stages*,

> Whoever has respect for their guru and
> With devotion consistently and enthusiastically offers respect
> And listens well is a pure disciple.

One must practice the sacred oral instructions of a holy guru endowed with the lineage. For this there are two methods:

1. How to Practice during the Actual Session
2. How to Practice during the Meditation Break

The first has three parts:

1. How to Begin the Session
2. How to Engage in the Actual Session
3. How to End the Session

The first also has two parts:

1. ENGAGING IN THE PRELIMINARY STAGE
2. HOW TO ACCOMPLISH THE BRANCHES OF YOGA

The first has five parts:

1. ARRANGING THE VARIOUS ARTICLES OF YOGA
2. GOING FOR REFUGE AND GENERATING BODHICHITTA
3. INSTANTANEOUS SELF-GENERATION
4. BLESSING THE INNER OFFERING
5. BLESSING THE [OUTER] OFFERINGS

Arranging the Various Articles of Yoga has two parts:

1. MOTIVATION
2. REQUESTING THE LINEAGE GURUS

As is stated in the *Direct Expression*,[22]

> In a valley or on a mountain peak,
> On the banks of a great river
> Or the shores of a great ocean,
> In a tree or a virtuous place,
> In the house of a female spirit or a charnel ground,
> In a variety of isolated places or
> In a temple or a stupa,
> In a house or at a crossroads,
> If a practitioner should accomplish yoga there,
> The fruits of all desires will be bestowed.

As it is said, because places like these might prove difficult for a beginning practitioner to endure, therefore, one should practice in a place that has been blessed by the presence of a holy person who had practiced there

---

22. Tib. *mNgon brjod*. This is an explanatory tantra.

previously, an isolated place that is free of all unfavorable conditions, such as noise and disturbances and commotion from humans and nonhuman beings alike, and that possesses all the favorable conditions, such as water, firewood, and so forth. In such an agreeable place or in a "house of accomplishment" that is under your control,[23] first sweep it, then burn excellent incense, and sprinkle cow products together with the five nectars. Face south and arrange a drawing of a variegated vajra under your cushion.[24] Above that spread flowers and arrange a soft cushion of *durwa*[25] grass. In the southern direction of your abode, facing you, set up either a statue or a painting of the deity Father and Mother, a text of the tantra, and [a stupa]; thus you will have arranged the three supreme supports.[26]

In front of these arrange a round torma made from clean barley flour with rice dough, peas, and white garlic; mix these together and mix the powder with nectar. Take water, beer, milk, and melted butter and shape them into a [round torma] made from clean pastry, encircled by four small ball tormas,[27] and smear these with paint and adorn them with a moon, sun, nada, and circle. To the left of this torma is the torma to the general dakinis, round and painted [red][28] with white and red ornaments.[29] In front of that are the offerings to the self- and front-generations, with the two waters and the close enjoyment offerings arranged in two rows beginning from the left of the object of the offerings. In front of you, beginning from the right [and going to the left] is a rosary made of either human bones or bodhi seeds, a hand drum, bell, vajra, inner offering, grains for

---

23. This is because if you do retreat in a house that is under someone else's control, they may ask you to leave before you complete your retreat.

24. These days it is said that you should place a swastika under your cushion to symbolize stability because a vajra is a hand symbol of the deity, and if you were to sit upon this, such an action would constitute a tantric downfall.

25. Durwa grass (Tib. *rtsa dur ba*) is a long multijointed grass. The main joints symbolize a stable and long life.

26. These are the three supports of the body, speech, and mind of a buddha. A statue symbolizes his body, a text symbolizes his speech, and a stupa symbolizes his mind.

27. Tib. *bshos bu*.

28. Tib. *dpa' bshos zlum po smug rtsi*.

29. In the Panchen Lama's sadhana on which Ngulchu Dharmabhadra is commenting here, there is no preliminary torma. Usually there are three tormas: the central one for the Father, Mother, and the four dakinis; the one to the left for the mundane guests; and the one to the right—not included in this commentary—that would be similar to the torma used for the preliminary torma. In the sadhana included in this text, the members of Zongkhar Chöde have added the preliminary torma to the sadhana. Therefore, for our purposes we need all three tormas.

tossing, and, if you have them, a katvanga, Brahmin thread, skull cup, bone ornaments, and so forth. [In this way] assemble the entire collection of [ritual] articles, and wear clean clothes.

Since it is even difficult for any of our great actions of virtue to become perfectly pure and free of being motivated by such mental afflictions as desire and hatred, not to mention the virtuous activities of secret mantra, we have to stop and immediately reflect on the defects of such false virtue as would be gained from all meditations on the yoga that follows while being under such an afflicted influence.

MOTIVATION

Contemplate, "Through the practice of Vajrayana I must quickly attain the state of a complete buddha in one short life of this degenerate age without waiting three countless great eons. I must complete the perfection of the realizations and the abandonments and attain the state of a complete buddha for the sake of all mother sentient beings." From within this aspiration of bodhichitta, recite the [verses from the sadhana] with at least a contrived motivation.

REQUESTING THE LINEAGE GURUS

If you are going to make request to the lineage gurus, at this point you should recite "Glorious Heruka..." and so forth. Furthermore, you should meditate that on the crown of your head are your empowering lineage gurus, stacked one upon the other. First, [the uppermost], is glorious Chakrasamvara with one face and two hands together with the Mother. Below him, imagine that all your lineage gurus, from Mahasiddha Ghantapa downward to your root guru, are all the nature of your own guru and in the aspect of Heruka with one face and two hands together with the Mother, seated on a lotus and sun cushion. This symbolizes that all of these gurus have attained the state of Heruka through relying on the path of this deity. Furthermore, as you recite the request to each one, nectar descends from the bodies of the gurus, washing your body inside and out, thereby purifying all sickness, harm from spirits, nonvirtues, and obscurations. The nectar fills your whole body and your life, merit, and good qualities all increase. While making this request, each of the gurus dissolves sequentially into the one below. Recite everything up to "May I receive your blessing to manifest the four bodies," and at the same time imagine that your own root guru dissolves into you.

Going for Refuge and Generating Bodhichitta

This has two parts:

1. Going for Refuge
2. Generating Bodhichitta

The first has four parts:

1. Visualizing the Object of Refuge
2. Establishing the Cause of Going for Refuge
3. The Actual Act of Going for Refuge
4. The Descent of Purifying Nectar

Visualizing the Object of Refuge

While visualizing yourself clearly in the aspect of a mahasiddha, imagine that in the sky before you is a square celestial mansion with four doors, complete with all the characteristics. In the center is a lion throne, a lotus, and sun cushions, resting upon Bhairava and Kalarati. Upon this is Chakrasamvara with four faces and twelve arms, together with the Mother. In the [four] directions are the dakinis and so forth, serving as the supported and supporting [mandalas]. From here downward, the visualization is in accordance with the explanation in the lamrim.[30]

Above the root face of the principal on the crown of his head is a lion throne, lotus, and sun seat. He is the nature of your own kind root guru

---

30. This means that, below the Heruka Father and Mother and the four dakinis, the rest of the object of refuge should be visualized in the same way as the object of refuge is taught during lamrim teachings.

in the aspect of conqueror Vajradhara, with a blue-colored body, one face, and two hands, holding a vajra and bell and embracing the Mother Vajradhatu Ishvari, who has a blue-colored body, holds a curved knife and skull cup, is adorned with eight jeweled ornaments, and wears silken garments. The Father sits in the vajra position and the Mother in the lotus position. Above him, from Yongzin Gugay Losang Tenzin[31] to just below the gilded roof of the celestial mansion,[32] beginning with Heruka, are all the lineage gurus just as visualized during the request, with the gurus stacked one above the other. In the space around the celestial mansion and the golden roof are the sutra buddhas, bodhisattvas, hearers, solitary conquerors, heroes, heroines, dharma protectors, and guardians. Upon the golden roof and inside the small house are the Dharma [books] of the four classes of tantra of the resultant Vajrayana and the Dharmas of the three vehicles of Sutra and so forth. It is said that you should clearly visualize the objects of refuge.

Establishing the Cause of Going for Refuge

To your right is your father, to your left your mother, behind are your relatives and friends, and in front are your enemies, harmful spirits, and ill omens and so forth; [thus] visualize the six classes of living beings. With a mind of fear and trepidation for all the suffering of samsara and the lower realms together with faith and confidence that the [Three] Jewels have the power to protect [you], imagine that the ground is shiny with a dark stain or shade.[33]

The Actual Act of Going for Refuge

Recite, "To the Buddha, Dharma..." up to "I will [always] go for refuge." The meaning of the rest is easy to understand. When we say "always" in

---

31. This is the guru from whom Ngulchu Dharmabhadra received the empowerment of Heruka.

32. Tib. *rgya phubs*. This is the small roof, layered with gold, that rests above the ceiling of the celestial mansion. Below this is a square opening, or skylight, through which the stacked lineage gurus emerge.

33. Tib. *sa'i dreg pa ltar smug shig ge yod par bsam pa'o*. Thanks to Sharpa Tulku for the translation of this verse.

the verse, "I will *always* go for refuge to Buddha, Dharma, and Sangha," this itself is a brief teaching on going for refuge six times a day.[34]

When we say, "To all three spiritual vehicles...," [this refers to] the principal subject matter of the hearer vehicle, which is the teaching on the four noble truths. The principal subject matter of the solitary conquerors is the twelve links of dependent origination. The principal subject matter of the great vehicle is [both] the vast and profound [lineages] of the sutra class.

When we say, "The yoga of secret mantra...," this refers to the four great classes of tantra.

When we say, "The dakini...," [we are going for refuge to the Dharma jewel]. As stated in the tantra *Ornamental Essence of the Vajra*,[35]

> The dakas and the dakinis of
> The tantra of the *Ornamental Essence of the Vajra*.

From among the tantras, this is principally teaching a yogini tantra and represents the Dharma jewel.

[Thus, when we] recite, "The heroes, heroines...," these are the tantric Sangha such as Khandakapala, Partzandi, and the rest of the heroes and heroines of the three wheels as well as the [goddesses] of the corners and the doors. The empowering goddesses are the four mothers together with Vajravarahi.

When we recite, "And the bodhisattvas...," this refers to the great beings, the bodhisattvas that are the sutra Sangha jewel. Then, when we recite, "Especially, [I will always go for refuge to my spiritual master]...," this represents going for refuge to the guru. The word *lopön* (Tib. *slob dpon*) translates the Sanskrit word *acharya*,[36] which signifies that he engages in teaching conduct. Also, since the root guru in nature is the condensation of all of the objects of refuge, it says "especially..." and means that he is *especially* that.

And when saying, "I will always go for refuge..." and so forth, it is

---

34. This refers to the tantric commitment to go for refuge six times each day.
35. Tib. *rDo rje snying po rgyan gyi rgyud*.
36. *Acharya* is a Sanskrit term and is commonly translated as "master" in English.

showing that even after I achieve buddhahood myself, it is necessary to rely upon this lord, my guru, and that it is totally improper to abandon him. It is taught that the root guru and the lineage gurus are primarily the Buddha refuge.

The Descent of Purifying Nectar

From the parts of the bodies of the objects of refuge, a stream of nectar descends, purifying all the nonvirtues and obscurations of yourself and all living beings in general and, in particular, the obstructions that interfere with your meditations on the quick path of the Vajrayana. All sicknesses, harm from spirits, nonvirtues, and obscurations are expelled in the aspect of feces, bloody mucus, spiders, scorpions, charcoal, smoke, and ash, and exit through the doors of your senses and all your pores, purifying everything. Your body transforms into the nature of clear luminosity and is completely filled with the nectar. Imagine that your life, merit, and so forth, and, in particular, all the good qualities compatible with your meditation on the quick path of the Vajrayana are generated in the mental continua of both yourself and others.

Generating Bodhichitta

"To accomplish the welfare of all living beings . . ." and so forth indicates striving for the welfare of others. "May I become Heruka . . ." indicates striving for enlightenment for both [oneself and others] and represents the generation of aspiring bodhichitta. "Sentient beings . . ." and so forth reveals that the purpose of practicing this path is to place all sentient beings in the status of Heruka and indicates generating engaging bodhichitta. "[And then lead] every living being [to Heruka's . . .]" indicates practicing the path to attain the state of Heruka, which represents the generation of engaging bodhichitta. "To Heruka's supreme state . . ." represents having the promise of aspiring bodhichitta. As it says in the *Samvarodaya*,

> Whereas the mind to benefit others is love,
> [Wishing] to destroy their suffering is compassion;

> For others to be satiated by bliss is joy,
> Equality toward other living beings is equanimity.

One must meditate on the bodhichitta endowed with the four immeasurables to attain the nonabiding nirvana of Brahma.[37] For the purpose of practicing the Mahayana, one must teach all paths. In that way it is taught that one must recite the refuge and bodhichitta prayer three times.

INSTANTANEOUS SELF-GENERATION

Recite, "In an instant I arise in the body of Heruka together with the Mother." Because you will not be able to bless the offerings, tormas, and so forth, with an ordinary appearance and conceptions, you must meditate on deity yoga.

The objects of refuge then collect inward by stages into the aspect of a blue light, which dissolves into you. Imagine that all the gross and subtle aggregates, the aggregates of flesh, bones, and so forth—the basis of imputation for the "I"—gradually dissolve until they melt completely into the aspect of blue light and disappear. By recalling the view of emptiness, collect ordinary appearances and conceptions that appear to the mind. Furthermore, imagine that the view of emptiness is mixed inseparably with the resultant-time exalted wisdom of nondual bliss and emptiness. This is the brief meditation on bringing death into the path of the truth body.

From within that state, in your place appear cushions of a variegated lotus and sun, upon which are Bhairava and Kalarati. The clarity of one's own mind of exalted wisdom of bliss and emptiness transforms into a cubit of blue light. Imagine clearly that this is the resultant-time enjoyment body. This is the meditation of bringing the intermediate state into the path of the enjoyment body.

This light grows more and more coarse, and you transform into Heruka, of whatever size is suitable to your mind. Heruka is dark like the color of a raincloud, with one face, two hands, and three eyes. In his right

---

37. Here the word "Brahma" could refer only to a bodhisattva on one of the pure grounds or a buddha, since a nonabiding nirvana is only in the continuum of one of these two.

hand he holds a golden, five-pronged vajra and in his left a bell made of white metal with a golden, five-pronged vajra handle; they are embracing Vajravarahi, who has a red-colored body, one face, and two hands holding a curved knife and skull cup. His right leg is outstretched, and his left one is bent. The Mother is in the lotus posture,[38] and her thighs wrap around the Father's thighs. The Father is adorned with six mudras and the Mother with five. Limitless light rays radiate from both bodies in all the cardinal and intermediate directions and pervade the extent of the mandala. Furthermore, you are not ordinary but are the actual resultant-time glorious Heruka. Think, "I am extraordinary in that I have eliminated all faults and completed all good qualities." Then generate stable divine pride as the emanation body. It is taught that in this state you should meditate on bringing rebirth into the path of the emanation body.

Blessing the Inner Offering

Recite the [section from the sadhana] for the blessing of the inner offering up to "blessed and [becomes vast]."

The *Samvarodaya* states,

> The mantra OM AH HUM
> Is always used for blessing.
> The mantra HA HO HRIH
> Is for purifying and realization.
>
> One should know that
> The letter HA captures color,
> The letter HO captures scents,
> The letter HRIH conquers power;
> One should rely upon this nectar.

At the place of the inner offering is a white wheel with eight spokes

---

38. Even though at this point it says "lotus posture," it should not be mistaken for the sitting lotus posture. Here both Heruka and Vajravarahi are standing, she with her legs wrapped around Heruka's waist, which roughly makes the shape of a lotus; hence, the name "lotus posture."

that is the nature of Vairochana. There is a small hole in its center where there is a white letter HO. Above this is a red, eight-petaled lotus, the nature of Amitabha. It covers the little hole in the wheel and at its center is a red letter HA, upside down on its head. Above the HO on a sun seat is a blue, long letter HRIH, with the *tsetrak*.[39] Visualize to the right of that is a white OM, to the left is a red AH, and in front is a blue HUM, and recite HA HO HRIH three times. [Imagine] that those letters melt by stages into light and then bless [the inner offering] as it dissolves into the substance matter. Recite the HA HO HRIH and sequentially visualize [first] that the color is purified and takes on the aspect of orange nectar. The impurities, defilements, and so forth, of scent and taste are cleansed, and the substance becomes pure as a crystal. Inadequate power is purified and is transformed into nectar endowed with a hundred flavors with the special power to develop uncontaminated bliss in the mental continua of the guests.

As you recite OM AH HUM three times, they dissolve into the [inner offering] so that no matter how much the guests partake, the nectar is inexhaustible; [therefore] imagine that it greatly increases. At the same time, if you feel you have the energy, visualize at your heart in the center of a moon mandala that you appear in your ordinary aspect. In front of you are your father and mother of this life, to the right are your relatives, to the left are friends, behind are your dearest loved ones. Surrounding them are all sentient beings. With this visualization, as you recite OM AH HUM the first time, imagine that all the negative karma and obscurations, accumulated by yourself and all other sentient beings, accumulated by body are purified. When you say it a second time, imagine that all the negative karma and obscurations accumulated by speech are purified. When you say it a third time, imagine that all the negative karma and obscurations accumulated by mind leave through all of your pores in the aspect of smoke and soot. By dissolving into the nectar, your nature transforms and you develop altruism and bodhichitta. You must remember this again and again as it is of the upmost importance to sustain this [mind of bodhichitta].

39. The *tsetrak* (Tib. *tsheg drag*) consists of two dots to the right of a seed syllable letter transliterated from Sanskrit.

According to the teachings you must do either the brief or extensive blessing ritual in conjunction with the visualization.

Blessing the Outer Offerings

This has four parts:

1. Cleansing [the Outer Offerings]
2. Purifying [the Outer Offerings]
3. Generating [the Substances of the Outer Offerings]
4. Blessing [the Outer Offerings]

Cleansing [the Outer Offerings]

Recite the section for blessing the outer offerings. As you recite the Kandharohi mantra, imagine that at your heart, appearing clearly as Heruka, is a moon disk upon which is a letter HUM together with the nada. From this, which is in the nature of the exalted wisdom of bliss and emptiness, arise countless red Kandharohis, each with one face and two hands holding a curved knife and skull cup. They leave through your right nostril and chase away all the obstructing spirits who abide [near] the offering substances, like a hawk chasing away small birds, to the furthest shore of the great ocean, rendering them unable to return.[40]

Next, imagine that the [Kandharohis] reenter through your left nostril and dissolve back into the letter HUM abiding at your heart. Imagine that Kandharohi is the nature of bliss and emptiness, and with her exalted wisdom she has the power to completely destroy all obscurations, so, needless to say, she has the power to destroy all outer harmful and interfering spirits.

---

40. Here, the great ocean refers to Buddhist cosmology, where Mount Meru is in the center of the universe surrounded by the four continents and a great ocean. Chasing the spirits to the edge of the great ocean is equivalent to chasing them to the furthest reaches of the universe.

Purifying [the Outer Offerings]

Recite the SÖBHAWA mantra for purifying. The two SÖBHAWAs mean "nature." The two SHUDDHAs mean "pure." SARWA means "all." DHARMA means "phenomena." AHAM means "I am." [Thus the mantra means], "All phenomena are pure in nature, and I am that pure nature." Then, the offerings together with the vessels melt into light and put an end to all impure appearances to the mind. Imagine that both types of conceptions of true existence dissolve into emptiness and that that very emptiness is then realized by your mind and is [the same nature as] the resultant-time great bliss. By doing this it is crucial to realize that all phenomena you generate throughout the sadhana will arise as the display of bliss and emptiness.

Generating [the Substances of the Outer Offerings]

Recite, "From the state of emptiness . . ." At that time at the place of the offering vessels,[41] each skull cup arises from the first letter of its name, KA, adorned with a drop (ཾ) on top. The KA symbolizes bliss and the drop, emptiness. This melts and instantly arises as a skull cup, white on the outside and red on the inside, as vast as the three thousand [worlds]. Inside this, the exalted wisdom of bliss and emptiness appears in the aspect of a letter HUM. This [HUM] melts and completely transforms into the water for the feet and so forth. The offering substances are the nature of extraordinary exalted wisdom of inseparable bliss and emptiness. Their aspect is the special offering substances, and each appears in its own form. Their special function is to be enjoyed when the guests partake of them through their tongues and as visual objects of the eyes and so forth. These objects have the power to generate uncontaminated, extraordinary bliss in the six senses. Imagine that they are endowed with these three special qualities [that is, they have the nature of bliss and emptiness in the aspect of the offering substances and operate as objects of the senses to bestow uncontaminated bliss and emptiness].

---

41. The translation equivalent of *kapala* is "bliss sustainer."

BLESSING [THE OUTER OFFERINGS]

Blessing is done with mantra, mudra, and meditation. First, recite, OM AHRGHAM . . . and so forth. Conjoin the names of the offerings with the seed syllables of the three vajras [OM AH HUM]. Augmenting the names of the offerings with these [three letters] and reciting them verbally while imagining that the nature of the three vajras is the essence of bliss and emptiness is blessing them with mantra. Performing the individual [hand] mudras is blessing them with mudra. Blessing them with concentration is represented by imagining that the three spheres—the object of the offering, the offering substance, and the person who makes the offering—are viewed as unobservable [that is, empty of inherent existence] and endowed with the three special qualities.

It is taught that if you wish to engage in the meditation and recitation of Vajrasattva, you should do so at this point.[42]

HOW TO ACCOMPLISH THE BRANCHES OF YOGA

This has four parts:

1. ACCUMULATING THE COLLECTION OF MERIT
2. BRINGING DEATH INTO THE PATH OF THE TRUTH BODY
3. BRINGING THE INTERMEDIATE STATE INTO THE PATH OF THE ENJOYMENT BODY
4. MEDITATING ON THE PROTECTION CIRCLE

ACCUMULATING THE COLLECTION OF MERIT

This has three parts:

1. INVOKING THE FIELD OF MERIT
2. COLLECTING THE ACCUMULATION OF MERIT
3. DISSOLVING THE FIELD OF MERIT

---

42. In the sadhana included in this book the Vajrasattva practice is inserted at this point.

INVOKING THE FIELD OF MERIT

Recite, "From the heart of myself appearing clearly as Heruka…" and so forth. At this point imagine that the eight petals of the heart-channel wheel are symbolized by a variegated eight-petaled lotus. In its center is a moon mandala, symbolizing the indestructible red and white drop at your heart. In the center of the moon mandala symbolizing the extremely subtle energy wind is the letter HUM, dark blue and standing upright. The *shabkyu*[43] [symbolizes] the exalted wisdom of accomplishing activities; the HA represents the exalted wisdom of discrimination; the head [of the HA], the exalted wisdom of equality; the crescent moon, the mirrorlike exalted wisdom; and the drop and nada, the exalted wisdom of the dharmadhatu. From the nature of these five exalted wisdoms, five-colored light rays radiate, completely filling the inside of your body and purifying the negative karma and obscurations that have been accumulated by your three doors since time without beginning. Your body becomes pure like a crystal egg. Light rays radiate out from all your pores and invoke, from Akanishta Pure Land, your guru in the aspect of Vajradhara, together with the collection of deities of Chakrasamvara's mandala. Furthermore, all the buddhas and bodhisattvas fill the space, like a pod is filled with seeds. Imagine they are invoked to the space directly before you, and the radiated light rays collect back into your heart. This symbolizes how all of samsara and nirvana are merely labeled by the mind, as the light rays and goddesses radiate out and collect back from the letter HUM at your heart. Finally, this symbolizes your extremely subtle wind and mind at your heart acting as the agent of these activities. When you gather these back and imagine that they dissolve into the HUM at your heart, this symbolizes the level of the completion stage wherein you dissolve all of the coarse winds and minds into the heart, which is the special ripening agent that gives rise to the clear light. This is a great and extremely profound quintessential instruction.

43. The *shabkyu* (Tib. *zhabs kyu*) is the hooklike curve at the bottom of the Tibetan letter HUM, representing the sound "u."

Collecting the Accumulation of Merit

This has three parts:

1. Prostration
2. Making Outer, [Inner, Secret, and Suchness] Offerings
3. Confessing and Rejoicing

Prostration

Recite, NAMO GURU CHAKRASAMVARA … NAMO [means] "prostration." GURU [means] "lama." CHAKRA [means] "wheel." SAM [means] "bliss." VARA [means] "supreme." SARWA [means] "all." DAKINI [means] "sky-goers." BHYA [indicates] the plural. Thus, it means "I prostrate to Guru Heruka Chakrasamvara and all the dakinis" and represents prostration. When saying this, imagine that all the sentient beings surrounding you are verbally reciting these words of praise together with you. Mentally make request with fierce devotion and respect. It is also taught that you should make prostrations, imagining that you are doing so with a number of bodies equal to the number of atoms in your body.

Making Outer, [Inner, Secret, and Suchness] Offerings

Recite, OM SARWA TATHAGATA … and so forth. At this time from the HUM at your heart, which is the nature of the exalted wisdom of bliss and emptiness—just as in the empowerment ritual of *The Essence of Great Bliss*—imagine that limitless offering goddesses holding offering substances emanate out and make the offerings.

The meaning of the offering mantra is as follows. OM consists of three parts: AH, U, and MA, which are the three vajras.[44] Those three letters, when they combine into the single letter OM, at one time become inseparable from the three vajras and the three spheres of the offerings

---

44. The three vajras are the vajra body, vajra speech, and vajra mind of a buddha, or by extension, all the buddhas.

and symbolize that they are mere nominal imputations and lack inherent existence.

SARWA means "all"; TATHA means "thus." GATA means "having gone." Together they signify having gone to the truth body through the suchness of emptiness and having gone to the form body through the suchness of the truth body. From AHRGHAM (water for drinking) to SHAPTA (music) are the offering substances. PRATITZA means "individual." SÖHA means "establish a foundation." When saying "Giving all things good, noble, and beautiful . . . ," although we are engaging many things, what we are requesting here [with SÖHA] is the bestowal of spiritual attainments. Furthermore, as for the offering substances that we have actually set out, reciting the offering mantra is the offering of mantra. Making the mudras with the hands is the offering of mudras. Emanating many [offerings] with the mind is the offering of concentration.

The offering of our practice influenced by the mind realizing that the three spheres lack true existence is an offering possessing the five characteristics; when the objects of the offering are satiated by uncontaminated great bliss, this is [related] to the vase empowerment.

The outer offerings, for their part, are related to the generation-stage path.

As [Mahasiddha] Ghantapa says,

> On the tongues of the bhagawan and the yoginis
> Arises a letter HUM and a three-pronged vajra;
> Imagine the assembly of deities are supremely satiated by enjoying the nectar that
> They extract through white tubes the size of a barley grain.

While reciting OM SARWA TATHAGATA OM AH HUM, imagine that from your heart emanate limitless red vajra-taste goddesses[45] holding skull cups, who scoop up the nectar and offer it to the guests. The inner offering is related to the secret empowerment and the path of inner-heat yoga.

---

45. These are vajra-rasa goddesses.

Concerning the recitation of the following, "Then Father and Mother enter into embrace…" and so forth, Ghantapa says,

> Have no doubt that this offering of the mudra
> Quickly brings attainments.

Imagine that, when the Father and Mother enter into embrace, the entire assembly of deities also experience simultaneously born great bliss. This, the secret offering, is related to the path of clear light and the wisdom empowerment.

By generating simultaneously born great bliss and emptiness, view the three spheres of the offerings as the display of bliss and emptiness. This is an unexcelled way to easily complete the two accumulations. The offering of suchness is related to the path of union and the fourth empowerment.

Although at this point saying PRATITZA is not in [some] texts, it is said that it is the intention of Mahasiddha Lawapa and Langka Gyalsang [that you should say PRATITZA in conjunction with the secret and suchness offerings]. You should apply the same reason for the ways of mentally engaging the meaning of this word in the offerings that follow.

Confessing and Rejoicing

Recite, "I go for refuge to the Three Jewels.…" Going for refuge is the "force of reliance" in dependence upon the objects of confession. Saying "And confess all negative actions individually…" is developing a "mind of regret" for all the negative actions that you and all sentient beings [have accumulated] in the past, like a person who has just ingested poison. Contemplate with a strong mind of restraint, "From here on out, though my life is at stake, I will not engage in [negative] actions." While considering each individual negative action over and over [in your mind], confess [each one] again and again.

When reciting "I rejoice in the virtues of beings…," [rejoice] in your own virtues and those of others accumulated throughout the three times and, like a poor person finding a treasure, rejoice with great joy.

When reciting "And accomplish a buddha's enlightenment…,"

although you are generating aspiring and engaging bodhichitta, if you were able to generate bodhichitta through mere recitation, then the other paths [to enlightenment] could also be accomplished that way and you would be able to generate all the paths to buddhahood in your mental continuum in one single day. Therefore, train your mind until you gain some experience. Then, if you wish to train in the bodhisattva activities elicited on the strength of that and the aspiration that has arisen from the depths of your heart, maintain the collection of the bodhisattva vows properly. This is what it means to perfectly train your mind in the practice of the six perfections.

[Doing all the activities above constitutes] the accumulation of merit. For example, if one is a womb-born human of this world, endowed with the six elements, who subsequently desires to take [rebirth] in the body of a god, because one will not transform into that in this life, it is necessary to accumulate [the necessary] compatible karma prior to that [next life].

Dissolving the Field of Merit

Recite, "The field of merit..." and so forth. Imagine that from the five parts of the letter HUM at your heart similar five-colored light rays radiate outward and, when they reach the field of merit, it dissolves sequentially inward from the edges into a blue orb of light and then dissolves between your eyebrows, thereby blessing your mental continuum.

Bringing Death into the Path of the Truth Body

At this point don't just merely recite the mantra in the text, [but] imagine that the contents and container [all worlds and the beings who inhabit them] dissolve into you and you also dissolve into unobservable emptiness. The recitation is said to be clarified for beginners. Therefore, at that time, with yourself appearing clearly as Heruka with one face and two hands, with stable divine pride, [dissolve all appearances and] manifest the clear light of the truth body of the buddhas. Next, to accomplish the welfare of others, you should develop the strong impetus to arise in the form bodies of the complete enjoyment body and the emanation body.

From the HUM at your heart, countless five-colored light rays radiate. From the hearts and joined organs of the Father and Mother [deities on the tips of those light rays], nectar is exuded outward, reaching all worlds and beings. They gradually melt into light and dissolve into you. You also completely melt into light and dissolve from above and below, like mist on a mirror, and dissolve sequentially into the HUM at your heart.[46] When the shabkyu of the HUM dissolves into the body of the HA, the earth element dissolves into the water element; the external appearance is the mirage-like appearance and the internal sign is like the body sinking into the earth. When the HA dissolves into the head [of the HA], the water element dissolves into the fire element, and the external sign is the smokelike appearance. The internal sign is the water element [of your body] and your lips, tongue, and so forth, becoming dry, with plaque building up on your teeth. When the head of the HA dissolves into the crescent moon, the fire element dissolves into the wind element, and the external sign is the firefly-like appearance in the sky. The internal sign is that the heat from the extremities begins to dissipate. As the crescent moon dissolves into the drop, the wind element dissolves into consciousness, and the external sign is the blazing candle-flame-like appearance. The internal sign is the stopping of the movement of the breath.

Imagine that all four of these signs arise. When the drop dissolves into the nada, the white bodhichitta at the channel wheel at the crown begins to break down; [it descends through the path of the central channel and] the path of white appearance [manifests]. Then, as the red element from the channel wheel at the navel begins to break down, the red element that is the nature of fire blazes upward and the mind of red increase [manifests]. When these two meet at the heart, the red and white elements are like two halves of a pea uniting, wherein the very subtle mind resides; at that moment the mind of black near-attainment arises. At the end of this there will be a period of unconsciousness without mindfulness. This period of unconsciousness is not a fault, but is a good quality because the deeper [the unconscious period], the more stable the clear light will be when it manifests.

---

46. In the following explanation by Ngulchu Dharmabhadra, he lists what are generally considered external appearances as internal appearances and internal as external. Why, I'm not sure. For an explanation of the standard listing, see Lati Rinpoche and Jeffery Hopkins, *Death, Intermediate State, and Rebirth* (Ithaca, NY: Snow Lion Publications, 1985).

When the nada also passes into the unobservable emptiness, one is awakened and released from the three faults. At this point the all-empty clear light manifests like the arising of a completely pure sky at dawn. This is the fourth of the four empties. At this time, the appearance of the nada is collected into clear emptiness. The experienced object is the immaculate bliss that is the nature of one's own mind. The mode of apprehension is the thought "not even an atom of all phenomena is inherently existent." For the factor of ascertainment, in the mind of the person realizing [emptiness] is divine pride established upon the thought "I am the actual resultant-time exalted wisdom of the truth body." You must have the four special features to establish divine pride.[47] In order to stabilize the divine pride of inseparable bliss and emptiness, it is excellent to verbally recite the mantra.

Concerning the meaning of the mantra, OM is the forerunner of the mantra. SHUNYATA is the objective emptiness. GYANA is the subjective exalted wisdom of great bliss. VAJRA means "indestructible" and represents the nondifferentiation of bliss and emptiness. SŌBHAWA means "nature." AMAKO means "nature or entity." AHAM means "I am." Together [it means], "I am the nature of the object emptiness and the subjective mind of inseparable exalted wisdom and great bliss."

At this point you should meditate on emptiness as follows: At the time of the basis, you purify the manifestation of the ordinary appearance of death that will arise. At the time of the path, the arousal of the example and meaning clear lights act as the ripening agents for your roots of virtue. Whereas example clear light still has very subtle dualistic appearances, meaning clear light has no subtle dualistic perception at all. Since it becomes the cause for accomplishing the truth body during the resultant time, this process is called "bringing death into the path of the truth body."

---

47. The four special features are (1) only emptiness appears without any conventional phenomena, (2) that emptiness is the lack of inherent existence, (3) your mind is experiencing spontaneous great bliss, and (4) upon the basis of these three, you recognize this as the resultant truth body of the deity and impute "I."

Bringing the Intermediate State into the Path of the Enjoyment Body

Recite, "Thus where all appearances…" and so forth. At this point you realize that you cannot just abide in the truth body and are impelled by the thought, "I must arise in the form body for the welfare of others." Thus recite, "From within the state of emptiness where all appearances have gathered, my mind is the truth body.…" With the wind as a vehicle acting as the substantial cause, it transforms into the [aspect of] the extremely subtle nada standing upright with three curves, white with a shade of red and abiding in space. With this, maintain the divine pride of being the enjoyment body. That [nada] symbolizes the subtle body of the intermediate-state being in which you will arise at the time of the basis and purifies the ordinary appearance of that intermediate state of becoming. At the time of the path, this functions to ripen the virtuous roots to accomplish the pure and impure illusory bodies. At the resultant time, this establishes the mental imprint to attain the resultant-time complete enjoyment body endowed with the seven qualities of embrace. This practice is called "bringing the intermediate state into the path of the enjoyment body."

There is a reason why it is necessary to establish this as soon as you arise from emptiness as the nada. As explained earlier, since womb-born humans of Dzambuling[48] are endowed with six elements and so forth, when these elements gradually dissolve, the clear light mind of death finally manifests. From the perspective of taking rebirth as a human, at the same time as the clear light of death ceases, the mind of black near-attainment of reverse order is accomplished. This is similar to the way an intermediate being, complete with hands and legs, is shot uncontrollably like an arrow either upward or downward; such is the intermediate state of becoming.

The purifying agent at the time of the path is accomplished by the skillful means of the completion stage until the final manifestation of the example and meaning clear lights that are similar to death. Through the power of the previous intention acting as the substitute cause for the intermediate state of an ordinary being, as the mind of black

---

48. Dzambuling is the Tibetan name for our world.

near-attainment of reverse order is accomplished, one is launched like an arrow being shot and impelled to accomplish the corresponding aspect of the illusory body complete with limbs.

The three curves of the nada symbolize the body, speech, and mind of the intermediate-state being. The white color symbolizes the fact that at the time of the basic intermediate state, as well as the path and the result, when the illusory body is accomplished, it arises from the basis of the life-supporting wind, which is white in color. The red symbolizes the basic intermediate-state being that is bound by attachment and symbolizes that, at the time of the path and the result, the minds of the two illusory bodies are bound by great bliss.

MEDITATING ON THE PROTECTION CIRCLE

Recite, "From the state of emptiness [comes a vajra ground]...." At that time, beneath the area of the celestial mansion is an extremely vast, variegated [double] vajra with either five or three spokes [in each direction]. All the intervening spaces are filled with tiny vajras lying down, while the vajra ground is filled with vajras like a gently gliding barley field.[49] The edge is encircled by tiny vajras. Upon this, standing upright is a vast fence rising upward, with the intermediate spaces filled with tiny vajras. It is round in shape like a Mongolian tent. Upon this is a vajra tent. The upper part is also like a Mongolian tent. There is a complete five-pronged vajra at its peak like a decoration. Between the fence and the tent, acting as a support, is a vajra canopy. There is not the slightest gap between all the [vajras], as if it were a single piece. It is sealed tight so that not even the tiniest particle of water could pass through. If you look, it is the nature of vajras, but if you touch it, it is as smooth as the surface of a mirror. Imagine that it is strong and stable and impenetrable, like a child in the womb that is unable to move,[50] indestructible and very hard and solid and able to withstand the wind at the end of the eon. The height of the protection circle reaches from Akanishta down to the wind mandala. It is so vast that

---

49. This is similar to a vast barley plain that is seen as one thing—that is, a field of barley—but upon closer inspection, it is evident that each space is occupied by individual stalks of barley.
50. Tib. *sreng me kyi bu'i mnas kyang.* Just like a child in the womb who is protected, imagine that the protection wheel is hard, solid, and protecting you from outer interferences.

it reaches the black iron mountain or, alternatively, for meditation you can make it whatever size you like

Beyond all of those vajras are also extremely wrathful fire sparks outside the tent and canopy, like the fire at the end of the eon. Going from the northeast it is white, yellow, red, green, and blue. The vajra fire goes in every direction, swirling in a blaze counterclockwise. Within this are the five-pronged vajra arrows, moving from above to below, from below to above, inside to outside, outside to inside, swirling like a tornado. While those on the dark side are not even able to look at it, those on the white side, on the other hand, perceive it as rainbow light.[51] Meditate in this way according to the sadhana, in order to dispel obstacles and interfering spirits.

How to Engage in the Actual Session

This has seven parts:

1. Generating the Seat for the Celestial Mansion
2. Generating the Supporting and Supported Mandalas by Taking Rebirth into the Path of the Emanation Body
3. Generating the Third "Manifest Enlightenment"
4. Generating the Fourth "Manifest Enlightenment"
5. Generating the Fifth "Manifest Enlightenment"
6. Visualizing the Stages of That Generation
7. Visualizing the Supporting Celestial Mansion

Generating the Seat for the Celestial Mansion

Recite, "In the center of this are the four elements stacked one above the other. . . ."

Ghantapa said,

> Wind, fire, water, earth, and the mountain,
> Square, sequential, with eight peaks:
> Meditate that they are all blazing with light as well.

---

51. The dark side and white side refer to evil and virtuous beings respectively.

Upon the vajra ground in its center is a blue, bow-shaped wind mandala, with its flat edge facing east. On both the right and left corners are vases with three-pointed banners, marked with living beings and victory banners coming from their mouths. Upon that is a fire mandala, red in color, in the shape of a triangle, with its single point facing east and its three corners marked by flames. Upon that is the water mandala, white in color and round in shape, its center marked by a vase filled with water. Upon that is the earth mandala, which is yellow in color and square in shape. Its four corners are marked with three-pronged vajras. Upon that is square Mount Meru; its nature is four precious substances: crystal in the east, lapis in the south, ruby in the west, and gold in the north. It is beautified by eight small peaks in the four cardinal and intermediate directions. In the center of Mount Meru comes the stem of a broad, sixty-four-petaled lotus of various colors: white, yellow, red, and green. It can also have either sixty-four, thirty-two, or sixteen [petals]. The center is green and the corolla is yellow. The distance from the outer edge of one lotus petal to another is eighty-four small-sizes in width.[52] The length from the outer edge of the center [of the lotus] to the other outer edge is eighty small-sizes [in width]. Upon that is a variegated vajra with three spokes in each [of the four] directions, making twelve in all, or [alternatively] five in each direction, making twenty in all. Whatever way you visualize it, the color of the spokes correlates with the directions.[53] The central spokes are blue and three large-sizes thick at the base, four large-sizes thick in the middle, and one at the tip. Each of the spokes is two small-sizes at the base, three in the center, and one at the tip. All the small spokes are sixteen small-sizes in length. The

52. In this section dealing with the proportions of the celestial mansion, there is a very simple means of measurement. The measurements are made according to the size of the principal deity. There are small-sizes, large-sizes, and door-sizes. A small-size is one cubit, which is the measure from the elbow to the tip of the middle finger of the principal deity. Therefore, if you have a deity that you imagine to be six feet tall, one small-size will be approximately eighteen inches. A large-size and a door-size are the same. They are equal to the extent of the outstretched arms of the deity, from the tip of the middle finger across to the tip of the ring finger of the other hand. This will be equal to the height of the deity, which, for the purpose of this explanation, is six feet. That being said, you could make your deity any size at all—whether one hundred feet or one inch—the measurements would adjust themselves accordingly, resulting in a proportionately sized celestial mansion.

53. Thus, the central spoke is blue, the eastern spoke is white, the northern spoke is green, the western spoke is red, and the southern spoke is yellow.

spokes in the directions come from the central spoke above the Brahmin line [running east to west]. From there in each direction, they each go eight small-sizes at the outer edge and six small-sizes at the inner edge. A small portion on the outside is bent upward, and the outer tips of the central spoke extend two small-sizes. The spokes in the cardinal directions as well as the [pearls] hanging from the mouths of the sea monsters symbolize not abandoning living beings through compassion.

The center of the variegated vajra with five spokes is five door-sizes in height, and the one with three spokes is one door-size [in height]. The shape of the center is square and flat and is twelve door-sizes in width. In the center of that is a variegated, eight-petaled lotus. The petals in the four directions are red, in the southeast and northwest, they are yellow, in the southwest, green, and in the northeast, they are black. The center is green and the corolla is yellow. This is the meaning of reciting, "In the center of a variegated eight-petaled lotus. . . ."

Furthermore, as cited in Lawapa's commentary,

> The petals in the directions such as in the east and so forth are [red] like sunlight; those of the southeast and northwest are yellow; that of the northeast direction is [black] like a charnel ground; the lotus is variegated with green [in the southwest] and dark blue.

Thus [visualize] according to this explanation.

Generating the Supporting and Supported Mandalas by Taking Rebirth into the Path of the Emanation Body[54]

The first manifest enlightenment is generating the two [sets of Sanskrit vowels and consonants]. Recite, "In the center are two sets of vowels and

---

54. This section of self-generation is also known as the "five manifest enlightenments." The first is manifesting the white vowels. This represents the mirrorlike exalted wisdom. The second is manifesting the red consonants, which represents the exalted wisdom of equality. These two do not have their own heading in our text. The third, the complete transformation of the HUM, symbolizes the exalted wisdom of discrimination. Light rays radiating from the letter HUM and enlightening all living beings symbolizes the exalted wisdom of accomplishing activities. And finally, there is the instantaneous manifestation of the supporting and supported mandalas from

consonants, the nature of the signs and indications [of an enlightened being] . . ." and so forth. At that time, the [two sets] of sixteen vowels in the center of the small variegated lotus are the nature of the thirty-two signs. The first sixteen begin in the east at the Brahmin line with A, go counterclockwise, and end at the western Brahmin line with AH. The next sixteen are arranged clockwise beginning in the east at the Brahmin line with A and ending at the western Brahmin line with AH. They are white in color and symbolize the white element obtained from the father that runs up the right leg from the tip of the right toe to the crown of the head, consisting of fifteen ascending parts and one stationary part—making sixteen in all. [The other set of vowels] symbolizes the fifteen descending parts and the one stationary part that run down the left side of the body from the crown of the head to the tip of the toe of the left foot.

In the *Samvarodaya Tantra* it says,

> From that, furthermore, the forms of the drops
> Are perfectly explained as moving,
> Beginning from the first white day[55]
> Until the full moon.
> On the first day of the white, the letter A—
> That letter is at the toe.
> Secondly, the letter AH is at the calves.
> Third, the letter I[56] at the thighs.
> The birthplace is the fourth—the letter IH.
> The navel is the fifth—the letter U.
> The heart is the sixth—the letter UH.
> The breasts are the seventh—the letter RI.
> The throat is the eighth—the letter RHI.
> The palm of the hand is the ninth—the letter LI.
> The cheeks are the tenth—the letter LHI.
> The eyes are the eleventh—the letter EH.

---

the moon, vowels, consonants, and HUM. Reciting the three instantaneous mantras symbolizes the exalted wisdom of the dharmadhatu.

55. Here "white day" refers to the fifteen days of the waxing moon and "black day" refers to the waning moon.

56. This is pronounced "ee." Apply this to the following letter pronounced "eeh."

The nose is the twelfth—the letter EIH.
The forehead is the thirteenth—the letter O.
The crown of the head is the fourteenth—the letter Ö.
The left is beer and the right fish,
And these are the nature of the letters AM and AH.

Beginning from the black day
Until the empty sky, they
Move in a similar fashion.

Distinguished by the waxing and waning moon, the stacking and the descent of the drops function to unify the thirty-two parts.

Beyond that are the thirty-four consonants, which are the nature of the eighty marks [of a fully enlightened being]. Add six [extra consonants] by adding two, THA DA; two, THRA DHRA; and two, YA and LA, and you end up with forty. "Each one should be understood as possessing the five elements. . . ." This means that they possess each of the five elements—earth, water, fire, wind, and space. For each of these, there is joy, supreme joy, extraordinary joy, and simultaneously born joy, and combining each of these four [with the five elements] makes twenty. Each of those twenty also have a particle of the red element obtained from the mother, thereby making forty. Each of those can be distinguished by method and wisdom, thus making eighty. This is the intention of Changkya Rinpoche in his commentary, *The Lamp Illuminating Great Bliss*. One row goes clockwise, and one line goes counterclockwise and is red in color. The vowels were perfectly arranged earlier. In the texts of Heruka the system of arranging the vowels and the consonants is out of order. Therefore, since this is very difficult for meditation, the tantra requires explanation. It is said that this tradition of arranging the vowels and consonants is comparable to the protection wheel of Yamantaka, as explained in the explanatory tantra, *Three Conceptions*.

The two sets of vowels and consonants completely transform into a moon mandala, white with a shade of red. The thirty-two white vowels are white, and the eighty red consonants appear very clearly like the reflection in a mirror. The white part of the color of the vowels and moon [symbolizes] the mirrorlike exalted wisdom of an enlightened being, and the red color of the consonants [symbolizes] the exalted wisdom of equality of an enlightened being. Therefore, according to the previous commentators, from the perspective of qualitative similarity with the basis of purification, the four elements and Mount Meru have a qualitative similarity with the outer bodies of the Father and Mother, where the intermediate-state being's consciousness is going to take rebirth. The small variegated lotus has a qualitative similarity with the two channel wheels [of the Father and Mother]. The white and red vowels and consonants have a qualitative similarity with the white and red elements. Meditating on the vowels and consonants completely transforming into the moon, white with a shade of red, has a qualitative similarity with the mixing of the red and white elements inside the womb.

Generating the Third "Manifest Enlightenment"

Recite, "I, the nada standing in space...." At that time the nada, in the nature of the enjoyment body, sees its place of rebirth, which is a white moon cushion with a shade of red. Contemplate, "While in this illusory body, ordinary beings are unable to see me with their eyes; therefore, I must enter into the coarse red and white bodhichitta of the buddha Father and Mother and take up the emanation body to accomplish the welfare of impure living beings." This thought impels the nada to enter into the center of the moon, which is qualitatively similar to the consciousness of the intermediate-state being entering into the center of the drops [of the Father and Mother]. Furthermore, in the beginning, the consciousness of the intermediate-state being, after the mixing of the sperm and ovum in the womb of the Mother, enters into the womb of the Mother and, having taken rebirth, begins to grow. As for the place of rebirth, it is said that [the intermediate-state being] enters the womb of the Mother below the stomach and above the bowels.

As for reciting "Gradually [the letter HUM]...," the drop and nada are the nature of Vajravarahi; below that, the crescent moon is the nature of Dakini. Likewise the head of the HA is the nature of Rupini. The body of the HA is the nature of Kandharohi. The shabkyu of the HUM is the nature of Lama. Imagine that the [letter HUM] becomes white with a shade of red.

The *Samvarodaya Tantra* states,

> In the center of completely pure
> AH LI KHA LI is the letter HUM,
> The nature of Vajrasattva.

The complete transformation of the HUM is the nature of the causal vajra holder and is the exalted wisdom of individual realization of an enlightened being. Furthermore, the sequential generation of the letter HUM has a qualitative similarity to the complete formation of the body inside the womb of the Mother. In the beginning, the outer shape of the embryo is like a circle, while the inside is very runny. Through the maturation process that occurs, a new wind is produced, and the fetus becomes thickened on both the outside and the inside like yogurt, but is not yet flesh. Through the maturation that occurs from that, a new wind is produced, and it becomes more solid but is unable to withstand pressure. Through the maturation that occurs from that, a new wind is produced, and the fetus becomes quite solid and can withstand pressure. Through the maturation that occurs from that, a new wind is produced, and the fetus develops limbs—the two thighs, the two shoulders, and the head—and in this way the signs of the five limbs become clear and prominent. Next, arising sequentially, are the hair, nails, and pores, as well as sense powers of the eyes and so forth, as well as the formation of either the male or female sign [the penis or vagina].

From the *Samvarodaya Tantra*,

> First, the [embryo] is runny;
> Oval is the second;
> Thickened is the third;
> Fourth it becomes hard.
> When signaled by the winds,
> It resembles a fish.
> From the seed of transformation of the fifth month,
> The five limbs are perfectly generated.
> The signs of the hairs, pores, and nails
> Are generated by the seventh month.

By the ninth month, the sense powers and forms
Are perfectly complete.

Generating the Fourth "Manifest Enlightenment"

Recite, "From the HUM, light rays radiate…." At that time, from the HUM, light rays of the five colors radiate above, below, and all around. On the tips of these light rays are limitless collections of mandala deities of Chakrasamvara that radiate, pervading all worldly realms. A pair of Heruka Father and Mother deities arrives at the crown of every living being, and from the point of their union, bodhichitta nectar descends and enters through the crowns of their heads. The two obstructions together with their imprints that have been accumulated since beginningless time are cleansed and purified. The nectar fills their whole bodies, and the Father and Mother deities dissolve [into all living beings] and establish them in the state of Heruka.

When reabsorbing the light rays, all the heroes and yoginis and so forth who have existed since beginningless time, abiding in all worldly realms in the ten directions, are hooked in the heart by the light rays and are invoked simultaneously to the space before you. Imagine that all the Father and Mother deities enter into embrace and become the nature of the play of the joy of passion. Imagine they arrive just in front of you, appearing clearly in the aspect of the letter HUM. Imagine that through the increase of their extreme passionate joy, the bodhichitta melts through the fire [of passion], and the drop that is the nature of bodhichitta melts and dissolves into the nada of oneself appearing clearly as the letter HUM, which becomes the nature of simultaneously born joy and is the exalted wisdom of accomplishing activities of an enlightened being. It is taught that at this point, it is very important that your visualization be stable and that you have generated a particularly strong experience of blissful joy in your mind.

Generating the Fifth "Manifest Enlightenment"

Recite, OM AH HUM … and so forth. This is the first of the three instantaneous mantras. By reciting OM AH HUM, remember the paths of the body, speech, and mind of the deity. The second [mantra] begins OM, which is the forerunner of the mantra. SARWA means "all." BIRA means "hero." YOGINI means "female yogi." KAYA means "body." WAKA means "speech." CHITTA means "mind." VAJRA is "indestructible." SÖBHAWA means "nature." ÄTMAKO means "reality." AHAM means "I am." While reciting, think, "I am the nature of the vajra body, speech, and mind of all the heroes and yoginis in the ten directions," and establish the divine pride of being the form body. Here, the great foremost being [Tsongkhapa] says one should reflect, "Since I have arisen in this body of Heruka that is the nature of simultaneously born great bliss, combining all deities, of course all the imperfect deities in Akanishta, Dzambuling, and so forth [are included as well]." This is an extremely important quintessential instruction from his sadhana, *Illuminating the Intention.*

In the third [mantra], OM has the same meaning as before. VAJRA means "indistinguishable." SHUDDHA means "pure." SARWA means "all." DHARMA means "phenomena." VAJRA is "indestructible." SHUDDHO is "pure." AHAM means "I am." While reciting this, develop the thought, "I am pure and my vajra-like mind of simultaneously born great bliss is inseparable from the lack of inherent existence of all phenomena." Thus establish the divine pride of being the truth body. The moon, vowels, consonants, and letter HUM melt into light, from which the supporting celestial mansion and the supported deities of the mandala, together with the eight charnel grounds, manifest. This is accomplished all at once. This meditation is the exalted wisdom of the dharmadhatu of an enlightened being. Furthermore, light rays radiating from the letter HUM and so forth have a qualitative similarity to the developmental stages of the channels, winds, drops, and limbs in the womb. Generating the supporting and supported mandalas simultaneously and mixing them into one symbolizes being born from the womb for the welfare of living beings into an impure environment among beings of those impure enjoyments. As long as your mind continues to take rebirth in an impure world among impure beings, your enjoyments will be under the power of karma and afflictive emotions. Therefore, train your mind in the meditations of this path.

Visualizing the Stages of That Generation

When unifying this with the completion stage, the four elements and Mount Meru symbolize the outer body of the practitioner. The center of the variegated lotus and so forth symbolize the channel wheels. The consonants symbolize the fire of inner heat, and the vowels symbolize the letter HAM at the crown of your head. Generating the white and red moon from those two symbolizes the melting of the letter HAM as a result of the blazing of inner heat. From the nada entering the moon up to the completion of the letter HUM symbolizes stabilizing simultaneously born great bliss by inducing the four joys of descent and ascent in dependence upon the melting of the HAM at the crown. This method symbolizes inducing the simultaneously born great bliss in dependence upon penetrating the vital points of the vajra body.

At this point, mother tantra explicitly reveals the method of [generating] simultaneously born great bliss. Furthermore, there is great meaning in the way the coarse emanation body arises from the illusory body and the way the supreme emanation body is generated from the enjoyment body and so forth.

The way both the supporting and supported mandalas are simultaneously generated from the moon, vowels, consonants, and letter HUM symbolizes accomplishing all at once the supported and supporting mandalas from the pure and impure illusory bodies. At this point, during the first stage [generation stage], this meditation becomes a unique ripening agent for our roots of virtue to generate the paths during the completion stage. At the resultant time, the complete enjoyment body arises from the final clear light of a learner as Heruka and accomplishes simultaneously the supporting and supported mandalas in their entirety. It is said that this deposits a unique imprint established through a similar and concordant aspect.

Visualizing the Supporting Celestial Mansion

Recite, "Furthermore, the celestial mansion..." and so forth. The center of the blue, square, variegated vajra that was generated earlier is [forty-eight small-sizes—that is, forty-eight cubits long and wide and twenty small-sizes high—upon which is the celestial mansion]. Measured on the inside, it is sixteen small-sizes [in floor space] on each side [of the central axis] in each direction [in other words, a square, thirty-two small-sizes on each side]. From the outer edge [of the floor space], there are five sequential layers of the wall, colored white, yellow, red, green, and blue, and [combined] they are one cubit in width and thirteen cubits in height.

In the center of each of the four sides are portals [made up of a vestibule and a porch, with the actual doors at the far end of the vestibule, opening out to the porch]. The outside [entranceway] of each [portal] is eight [small]-sizes in [width]. The side walls of each vestibule (*sgo khyud*), from the [inner] edge of the mansion wall to [the vestibule's] far end, are four small-sizes [long]. To the right and left [of each entrance hall], the back walls of each porch (*sgo 'gram*) are two small-sizes [long], and, going further outward [away from the center of the mansion], the side walls of each porch (*sgo logs*) are [also] two small-sizes [long].

[Jutting yet further outward from the center of the mansion,] on the frontward-facing [one-small-size-wide] edge of those right and left [side walls of each porch] are [jamb post] pillars, one small-size in thickness and eight small-sizes high [on its inner flank], two on each side [of the mansion], flush with the walls [of the porches]—in other words, planted onto them. [Resting] on top [of each pair] of them [across the entranceway] is a lintel (*gdung*), one small-size in height and thickness, beveled (*gsogs ka can*) [on each end], eight small-sizes in length [on its bottom surface] across the inside [of the entranceway] and ten small-sizes in length [on its top surface] across the outside [of the walls of the entranceway].

Supported on top of that [lintel] is a four-small-sizes-high continuation of the five-layered wall, which encircles [the entire mansion] without any gaps. Upon that [entire encircling wall] is an amber-colored jeweled frieze or molding (*pha gu*), one small-size in height and one and one half small-size in thickness with half [a small-size] protruding [from the wall on the outside of the mansion] and beautified with square, triangular, and other-shaped jewels of various colors that augment its beauty.

On top of that [molding] is a quadruple colonnade, with each [of its four stacked colonnades] consisting of a seven-part [entablature, with each part of the entablature made of a different] precious gem [or precious metal]. In more [detail], on top of the molding, in outer and inner [rows], is [a stack of two entablatures, one atop the other,] one every small-size space. [Each entablature] is made up of (1) a stacked amethyst column, with (2) a red pearl capital atop it, and (3) a *karketana* gem abacus (*gzhu*) atop that, with (4) two small crystal columns [standing side by side] on the top surface [of the abacus, each] with (5) a beryl capital atop it and (6) a silver abacus atop that. Propped up by the string of these capital structures, lying flat all along [the top of] each of the two stacked [entablatures] in the outer and inner rows, is (7) a golden cornice strip [*gser gyi ske rags*]. Thus, there are four [entablatures] like that, stacked [two by two in outer and inner rows], altogether two small-sizes high. At the corners [of the mansion, the quadruple colonnade] must be constructed with such things as the [*karketana* gem] abacuses [in the two rows] arranged crisscrossed, and so on.

On top of that [quadruple colonnade, extending one small-size beyond the walls] are the rafters (*lcam*) that support the outdoor terrace (*phyi kyams*) of the square [first-story] roof (*thog*). [There are twenty-eight such rafters on each side of the palace.] The outer ends of those [rafters], which extend [in the manner of the eaves] one and a half [small]-sizes out from the golden ledge (*gser snam*) [of the cornice strip], a half small-size thick and high, [have a half small-size between them, and] are fashioned such that that they have sea monster (*chu-srin*) faces [on them]. From their [mouths] hang loops (*dra ba*) and strands (*dra phyed*) [of precious gems]. As for the loops, they are two curves of strings of precious gems, arranged in rows and [strung] hanging down from mouth to mouth of the sea monsters. As for the strands, they are three or five strings of gems, hanging vertically down from the center of [the sea monsters'] mouths. On the tips of those [strands], for instance, when there are three [of them], there are such things tied on with golden [thread] as yak-tail fans with handles made of jewels or gems [on the outside two strands] and a small bell [on the middle one]. In the cases when there are five [strands], from the central one there hangs a jewel; from the two on either side of it, a little pennant (*'phen chung*) made of assorted fabrics; and from the two to the sides of those, flower garlands.

On top of [the one-and-a-half-small-size-long portion of] those [rafters that extend out from the walls], there are smaller rafters (*lcam thung*), each two small-sizes in length and a half [size] in thickness and width, with a half small-size [of its length] extending out [beyond the rafters. They are at the same level as the half-small-size-thick adobe roof and also have a half small-size between them.] On top of them is a very thin gutterlike strip (*bya 'dab*), also two small-sizes in length, encircling [the perimeter of the entire roof so that the eaves structure has no empty] spaces between the smaller rafters. From their outer ends, there hangs down one-small-size-[long] white drip ornament (*shar bu*), in shape like an upside-down ceremonial vase (*spyi blugs ma*), but without its lip, or the broken end of a bone, white. Above them are the one-small-size-[wide upright] white dentils [of the parapet] (*mda' yab*), a half [small-size] in thickness. They are one small-size wide and have the shape of half lotus petals, arranged in a row.

In the middle of the two flanks (*dpung*) of parapet dentils, above and to the right and left of the portal structures are [two] golden vases with a victory banner rising out [from one of them] and a streamer [rising out from the other], such that each wing is marked with two [vases, one] of each type, making eight of each. Above the parapet dentils on the four corners [of the mansion] are white parasols, with handles and top ornaments, six small-sizes [high], held aloft by monkeys who are facing inward. Along the rim of the parasols' spread is draped [a fringe] of dripping-down loops and strands of gems.

[Starting] from the edge [of the side walls of the vestibules], the bottoms of the walls are encircled [on their outside] by red ledges for [offering] desirable objects (*'dod snam*), two small-sizes in height and width. To the left of the eastern [portal, when right and left are reckoned from the point of view of] facing inward, are a blue lute goddess strumming a lute and a yellow flute goddess blowing a flute, and to the right, a red hand-drum goddess beating a round *mritange* drum and a green kettledrum goddess beating a large clay pot *muraja* drum. To the left of the northern [portal] are a red smiling goddess with her two [hands held in the] vajra fist mudra displayed at the outside [corners] of her mouth—in other words, placed on her two cheeks, in the smiling pose—and a blue flirting goddess resting a vajra and a bell on her hips in a haughty manner. To the right are a yellow song goddess playing thumb cymbals and a green dance goddess making the lotus-swiveling mudra. To the left of the western [portal] are a white flower goddess holding a vessel of flowers and a smoke-colored incense goddess holding a vessel of incense. To the right are an orange butter-lamp goddess holding a vessel with a flame and a green scented-water goddess holding a ritual conch shell of scents. To the left of the southern [portal] are a white sight goddess holding a red mirror and a red taste goddess holding a vessel of mead. To the right are a chartreuse touch goddess [holding] a length of multicolored cloth and a white phenomena goddess holding a dark blue, [upside-down, tetrahedral-shaped] phenomena source. These are the sixteen goddesses of pure awareness that make offerings to [the figures in the mandala].

The [near and far] corners [of the ends of these ledges where], outside [the mansion], the entrances [into the main hall] and the sides of the vestibules [meet], as well as [the near and far sides of the ledges] outside the corners of the walls, and also the floor inside [the mansion at those] corners—each of them is bedecked with a white crescent moon, with a red, eight-faceted jewel on it and a golden, five-spoked vajra standing upright atop that.

Below [each of] the [four] eleven-tiered archways (*rta babs*), fixed to [the twenty-small-size-high sides of the square, box-shaped, blue] hub of the crossed, double-vajra [platform, on which stands the mansion], is a staircase. [In the case when the crossed, double-vajra is] five spoked, there are twenty steps, with each one being one small-size in height, [sixteen small-sizes wide] and three-quarters of a small-size deep. [In the case when the crossed, double-vajra is] three spoked, there are four stairway landings [with the fifth landing being the archway platform that extends three small-sizes out beyond the mansion platform. Each landing is four small-sizes high, three deep, and sixteen wide. Each of the five flights of stairs consists of two ladderlike staircases of four steps each, going up in the middle of the right and left sides of each landing block], with each of the [twenty] steps being one small-size in height and a fraction of the three-small-sizes-[depth of each landing block]. The height of the [five] stairway landings for the two [ladderlike staircases, taken all together,] is like that of the hub of the [crossed, double-]vajra [platform, namely, twenty small-sizes high], and is three small-sizes deep.

In the drawn [mandala], the determination of the color to be painted on the space inside [the vajra spokes, between the spokes and] the archway, should be decided according to the influence of the color of the staircase of its own [direction] that would be visible. Considering that [point], then in the case of there being a three-spoked, [crossed, double-vajra platform,] it needs to be investigated whether, due to the influence of there being too little space for [including inside the painted spokes of the vajra the entire width of] the staircase, just two tiny parts of the upper blackened empty tier (*mun snam*) [of the seventh tier of the archways that stick out beyond the drawn spokes] should be the green color of the seed head of the variegated lotus [on which the crossed, double-vajra platform stands] that would be visible [and not black like the rest of that empty space]. Also concerning that, from the influence of the archways being three door-widths, [that is, twelve small-sizes high, rather than sixteen as in the case of the Guhyasamaja and Vajrabhairava mandalas,] I think that only in the [eleven tiers] being one door-width [in height, rather than two,] is there any difference.

On top of [and along the three-small-size-deep] right and left [sides of each] of the uppermost stairway landings, [which serve as the archway platforms,] are plinths with a square [cross section, one small-size high and wide, and] three small-sizes in depth. Atop these plinths are pillars, [three small-sizes high,] sticking out from [one-small-size-high] vases. The pillars are thin at their bases and crowns and are swollen in their middles, like the handle that supports a large two-headed vertical drum, one small-size thick [in the middle]. There are two of these [vases with pillars] on the right and left sides of each [archway platform], arranged in a row [perpendicular to the mansion walls] on the outer and inner [sides of the archway], with a one small-size empty space between them. [The outer side refers to the side further away from the center of the mansion, while the inner side refers to the side closer to center of the mansion. Thus] the height of the plinths, together with the vases and pillars, is five small-sizes. The staircases, vases, and pillars are the colors of the directions they are in [namely, white in the east, yellow in the south, red in the west, and green in the north].

[As for the eleven tiers of each archway,] atop [each of these sets of two] pillars there are (1) a yellow golden slab resembling a capital [spanning both pillars], (2) [a slab of white] pendants as [described] before, (3) [a slab] resembling the [amber-colored] molding of precious gems, and (4) a green horse-hoof [slab] (*rta rmig*) having drawings of horse hooves. Within the two blackened empty tiers, (5) upper and (6) lower, the pairs of pillars, arranged in a row [perpendicular to the mansion walls] on the outer and inner [sides of the tiers below them], are the colors of the directions they are in. Because the spaces of the upper and lower blackened tiers that are in between slabs are empty, they are black [in color] when they are to be drawn. In the spaces between the pillars [in the two blackened empty tiers] and the inner fringes (*khyog po nang ma*) of the archways, eight-limbed griffins, peacocks, swans, and female celestial singers are stacked [as well]—in other words, standing there, they also hold up the slabs [of the archways above them]. (7) The *varanda* slab [between the two blackened empty tiers] has the pattern of zigzag strips of assorted colors. On top of the upper blackened empty tiers are (8) [slabs of] pendants, (9) moldings, and (10) horse-hoof [slabs], similar in shape and color as [described] before [except that these now are single slabs extending over the entire archways, rather than two small slabs on either side of the archway entrances].

[Atop these upper horse-hoof slabs] are (11) outer and inner rows of upright dentils, ten each, as [described] before [a half small-size thick]. Atop the middle six [pairs of dentils] are flat slabs that cover their tops. In the middle of those [slabs], on lotus and moon discs, are golden [Dharma] wheels, with twelve or eight spokes. The hub together with the spokes [of each wheel] has a width of two small-sizes, and they stand [erect]. At a distance of a small-size to the right and left of them are a male and a female deer in the kneeling-down posture, with their heads uplifted—in other words, looking at the [Dharma] wheel. Their height, including their necks, is just one and a half small-sizes. The level plains [in between the two rows of upright dentils] in the first and second small-sized units, counting further out from the tails of the pair [beyond these slabs], are covered over by [the second tiers of outer and inner rows of] upright dentils, two in each [row], so that [the space between the two rows] is narrowed. In the two corners on top of the outer [small-sized units of these second tiers of dentils] are golden vases with a victory banner rising out [from one of them] and a streamer [rising out from the other]. On top of the inner [small-sized units of these second tiers of dentils], held aloft by monkeys who are facing inward, are parasols, having at their peaks [as top ornaments] a new moon, jewel, and vajra, and [draped] with a white cover having a [top row] of triangular ribbons with tassels [on their tips]—all together, two small-sizes [high]. Their jeweled handles are three small-sizes [long].

Atop [the outside ends of] the two [tiers] of horse-hoof [slabs] and the *varanda* [slab] are victory banners and streamers [rising out from golden vases], two on each [end of each of these slabs], on their outer and inner sides. The lengths and thicknesses of the [eleven tiers of] slabs are as [specified] in the root text on the [mandala's] blueprint. The depth [of each slab] is three small-sizes [the same as the archway platform].

On the leftover [empty strips, five small-sizes wide], on top of the hub of the crossed double vajra, beyond the ledges for [offering] desirable objects to the right and left of the archways, are [golden] vases. The width of their bellies and their heights are each one door-width [in size]. Rising out from them are wish-granting trees, having central [clusters of branches] and [below them] six branches on their sides. On the central [cluster of branches of each tree is perched] a red householder holding a jewel. At the ends of the six [lower, side] branches [of each tree] are an eight-spoked golden wheel, an eight-faced blue jewel, a sixteen-year-old pale blue maiden, a six-tusked white elephant, a noble green steed, and a black general complete with armor and wielding a sword and a spear. In the sky above the trees are greatly accomplished siddhas having the six [bone] ornaments. Also there are gods with [the upper] half of their bodies protruding from clouds, holding flower garlands causing a rain of flowers to descend upon the mandala.

As for the way in which the [ceiling and] roof are constructed, it is as follows. On the floor inside the [eight-door-widths-wide] celestial mansion is an eight-petaled variegated lotus, which from outer edge to outer edge is seven door-widths [in diameter]. The seed-head in its center is two door-widths [in diameter]; the [encircling] inner whirl of the corolla is one small-size [wide]; and the petals are each two door-widths [long]. As explained in the case of the variegated lotus that is the base for the celestial mansion, [the entire lotus is encircled by] a one-small-size-wide rim [consisting] of a blue rim together with a garland of vajras.

On [that] rim [of the variegated lotus on the mansion floor], directly in front of the [four] entrances [to the main hall], are planted eight pillars, two in each direction, a little less than four small-sizes to the right and left of the vertical and horizontal "Brahma" axes [of the mandala's blueprint grid]. The pillars are square in shape, one small-size thick, and the colors of the directions they are in. Those in the east are marked with wheels, those in the south with jewels, those in the west with lotuses, and those in the north with swords. Including their capital (*bre*), shorter abacus (*gzhu thung*), and longer abacus (*gzhu ring*), they are fifteen small-sizes high.

On top of those [eight pillars], over their blue base [namely, directly over the blue rim around the variegated lotus on the mansion floor], is a round circular beam (*gdung zlum*) [along the ceiling, with a square cross section] one small-size thick and marked with a garland of vajras. Also [on top of those eight pillars are] four crossbeams (*gdung*), level with, and similar to, [the circular beam in thickness,] making the pattern of a [nine-box] crosshatch (*mig mang, re'u mig*) from pillar to pillar. The ends [of these crossbeams] jut through the circular beam [and extend beyond to the walls].

In the four corners of the ceiling, both inside and [extending a little ways] outside [the mansion] are multicolored diagonal rafters (*zur lcam*), half a small-size high and a small-size thick. Their inner ends stick one small-size inside of the square central box [of the crosshatch formed by the four crossbeams]. Taking as an example the southeast diagonal rafter, the eastern half [of its length] is white and the southern half is yellow.

Each side of the outdoor roof terrace is propped up on twenty-eight rafters [perpendicular to the wall, a half small-size wide and a half small-size thick, with a half small-size between each of them. Their bottom sides are level with the bottom sides of the four crossbeams.] The way in which the outer ends of those [rafters] are set on top of the [upper] golden cornice strips [of the quadruple colonnade to form the protruding rafters and eaves] has already been explained. Their inner ends are propped up against either the diagonal rafters or the round circular beam. [The central rafters of each side of the mansion, like the diagonal rafters, stick a little inside the square central box formed by the cross-hatched main beams.]

Moreover, on the outer ends of these rafters [protruding outside the mansion walls], on the circular beam, and on the [four] crossbeams—the inner portions of which, within the circular beam, serve as supports for the square open pavilion (*rgya mthongs*) [on the roof]—and on the [inner] ends of the rafters that are supported against [the circular beam and the diagonal beams] to the right and left of the crossbeams [of each directional side] are jewels, adorned with joy-swirls (*dga' 'khyil*).

Above the left and right side walls of the outer and inner [ends] of the vestibules, a pair of beams, one small-size [thick], stretch across [the ceilings] between [these walls, above] the two top golden layers [of the cornice strip of the quadruple colonnade along these side walls], except for a little bit [that protrudes outside]. In between those two [beams across the vestibules], four rafters also stretch across [the vestibule ceilings parallel to these beams. Perpendicular to the outer one of those two beams, eight rafters stretch across the porches and protrude a little ways beyond the entranceways. Each of these twelve rafters is a half small-size wide and a half small-size thick, with a half small-size between them.]

The roofs of the porches (*sgo khang*) are constructed [as follows]: On top of the continuity of the [mansion] walls, moldings, and quadruple colonnades (*rtsig rgyung*) that are above the side walls of the porches (and above the entranceways), they are propped up on outer ends of rafters [that rest on those colonnades in the manner of protruding eaves. They are propped up as well on] the inside ends of the rafters [inside the entranceways and porches, the outer ends of the rafters that protrude on top of] the right and left back walls of the porches, and the beams in between them. A half-small-size-[thick layer of] adobe (*dral 'dam*) evenly covers the entire [ceiling of not only the porches, but also the vestibules and the areas inside the mansion between the walls and the square central box of the crosshatch formed by the four crossbeams. This one-small-size-thick ceiling, then, is made up of the half small-size of the rafters and the half small-size of adobe.]

Below the outer beams above [and across] the vestibule side walls [are the double doors to the mansion], with two door jambs (*sgo 'gram*) [on their sides], a lintel (*ya them*) [across their tops], and a doorsill (*ma them*) [across their bottoms, forming] a rectangular [doorframe] a half small-size wide. The door jambs are thirteen small-sizes in height [the same as the height of the walls]. The two-small-size width of the panels (*sgo glegs*) of the two doors each includes a little remainder [for the half small-size of the door jamb since the actual width of each panel is one and a half small-sizes]. Their heights are a little less than thirteen small-sizes [since the thirteen small-sizes includes a half small-size each for the lintel and doorsill]. Each half [of the double doors] is open outward and [both the doors and the doorframes] are the colors of the directions they are in. Arranged in each of the [two] small-sizes of height between the beams [across the rear of the vestibules] and the lintels [of the doors] are two rows of two white wheels in the east, yellow jewels in the south, red lotuses in the west, and green swords in the north, stacked on top of each other, with small spaces [between them], a quarter of a small-size in thickness, with nothing [in them].

Rising up on the inner ends of the diagonal eaves [that protrude inside the six by six small-size square central box of the crosshatched cross-beams] are posts [that lean inward] on a slant (*gseg ka can*), one small-size in thickness. They are twelve small-sizes in length and, of the four [posts] that are planted [on the diagonal eaves like this], two lean in facing east and two facing west. [Each pair] has two small-sizes [between them at their upper ends], so that they do not touch [each other]. Propped up on them is an [oblong] slab (*gdung leb*), running north to south, four small-sizes wide, one small-size thick, and ten small-sizes long. On the two [short] ends of this oblong slab in the north and south are garuda heads, with strands and loops of precious gems hanging from their mouths. Going up nine small-sizes from the bottoms of the [four slanting] posts, in the spaces [between the two pairs of posts] are two collar-beam crossbars (*bkag gdung*), going north and south, one between the two posts that slant in eastward and one between the two posts that slant in westward. Together with the slanting posts that they connect, they make the two H-shaped braces (*rgyab dbyig*) for supporting the pitched roof structure of the open pavilion on top of the ground story flat roof.

The open gap (*kha-gdangs*) of the square [inner box] of the crosshatch [made by the four crossbeams] is bounded by four small pillars [on each side], which, together with their capitals, shorter abacuses (*phul*), and longer abacuses, are five small-sizes high. [Horizontal] cornice beams [propped up by them] in the four directions make a square [bottom end of the frame for the four sides of the pitched pavilion roof].

In the corner spaces between the collar beam crossbars of the [slanting] posts are erected four slanting beams (*gdung 'khyog*) [that form the sides of the frame for the pavilion roof]. Their outer [bottom] ends are propped up on the four corners of the [square ring of] cornice beams [that form the bottom ends of the frame].

On top of those [beams of the roof frame] are short ribbing rafters that extend the distance across the span [of the frame. Part of the thicknesses of the ribbing rafters sticks out and runs along the outside of the roof panels.] These [ribbing rafters along the east and west sides of the pavilion roof] have the shape of lines with an obtuse angle (*gug*) in their middles [such that the east and west roof panels have two pitches, with the upper sections having a more severe pitch than the lower sections].

For the roof panels in the east and west [beneath the long ends of the oblong slab], the inner [upper] ends [of the ribbing rafters] are propped up on either the oblong slab or the corner slanting beams [of the roof frame]. The outer [lower] ends of the ribbing rafters are propped up on the cornice beams along the upper open gap [formed by the columns that ring the lower open gap of the crosshatched crossbeams of the mansion].

For the construction of the roof panels in the north and south [beneath the short ends of the oblong slab], the inner [upper] ends of the ribbing rafters are propped up on either the corner slanting beams or the collar beam crossbars [of the H-shaped braces. Thus, the spaces between the collar beam crossbars and the short ends of the oblong slabs, below the garuda heads that stick up from the oblong slab, are open.] The outer [lower] ends of the ribbing rafters are propped up on the square [ring] of cornice beams.

The outer [lower] ends of all the ribbing rafters extend a little ways past the [square ring of] cornice beams and are fashioned with sea monster faces [at their ends], with loops and strands [of precious gems] and so on hanging from their mouths.

Around the [outer, lower] perimeter of the [golden] pitched roof of the square blue [open pavilion], the upright dentils, like [half] lotus petals, stand erect and, hanging from a feather-thin gutterlike strip, pendants hang down.

In the center of the oblong slab on top [of the pitched roof] (*rgya phub*) is a small, rectangular, box-shaped cupboard (*khang bu chung*), three small-sizes wide and two small-sizes high, made of precious gems, in which is placed *The Root Tantra of Chakrasamvara*. On top of that is a nine-faceted gem adorned with assorted precious gems, and on top of that, [the structure] is completed with a five-spoked vajra [standing upright]. Each of these two is one small-size [high].

Thus, adding together the half small-size of the diagonal rafter, plus the ten and a half [small-sizes perpendicular height] when one and a half small-sizes are subtracted from the [twelve-small-size] length of the slanting posts [of the H-frame braces], plus two for the oblong slab and two for the top [crowning gem and vajra] makes sixteen [small-sizes]. Adding that on to the sixteen small-sizes of height of the inside [of the ground floor] of the celestial mansion [thirteen for the walls, one for the molding, and two for the quadruple colonnade, and not counting its ceiling structure of rafters and adobe] makes thirty-two [small-sizes]. And, as the floor space between the inside face of one wall to the inside face of the [opposite] wall is [also] thirty-two small-sizes, [the celestial mansion] is famed for having an equal width and height.

The way of constructing the roof is not clear in the great treatises about these [structures]. Nevertheless, although there are many slight discrepancies in the explanatory lineages, what has been related here has been according to the Ensa oral lineage and the glorious Segyu spoken lineage.

Beyond the vajra fence and fire mountain [are the charnel grounds]: in the east, Chanda-ugra—"Fiercely Ferocious"; in the north, Girigahvara-unnati—"High Mountain Jungle"; in the west, Vajra-jvala—"Blazing Vajra"; in the south, Kankalin—"Having Skeletons"; in the "powerful" [northeast], Ugra-hasya—"Ferociously Cackling"; in the "fire" [southeast] Mangala-vana—"Auspicious Forest"; in the "truthless" [southwest], Tamogra—"Dark and Ferocious"; and in the "wind" [northwest], Kilikili-ghosha-nadita—"Resounding with the Cries 'Kili Kili.'"

In these, beheaded corpses are roaming about, bodies gagged and hanged are standing, those that have fallen to the ground are lying down, and those that are impaled on spears are sitting. When engaging in these actions, [corpses] are engaged in the four types of actions like that. Other than those, dismembered bones and [skeletons that have] not been dismembered lie all about, strewn helter-skelter—thus are the charnel grounds.

As for the eight trees situated in the charnel grounds, they are the following: in the east, Shirisha; in the north, Ashvadatha; in the west, Kankela; in the south, Chuta; in the "powerful" [northeast], Pratra; in the "fire" [southeast], Karanja; in the "truthless" [southwest], Pataparka; and in the "wind" [northwest], Parthiva. The [order of the] directional protectors and so forth goes counterclockwise in the directions and clockwise in the intermediate directions. Except for this difference, then, as it is clearly explained in the words of the commentaries, I shall not explain them [here]. The manner in which the charnel grounds like that symbolize the stages of the path of the common vehicle from impermanence up to superior seeing and the uncommon paths of the complete stage should be learned from the expository commentaries (*dmar khrid*) on the generation stage of the Luipa [tradition of] Heruka and so forth.

The ceiling and floor inside the celestial mansion that is like that are white in the east, green in the north, red in the west, yellow in the south, and blue in the center. On the seed head of the variegated lotus in the center of the celestial mansion is a sun mandala, which is a flat red disc, equal in width to the variegated lotus's seed head. Visualize the inner whirl of the corolla a very slight distance from the edge of the sun mandala. Imagining that they are all established from features of the exalted wisdom of the principal figure, glorious Heruka, is said to be the most important essential point.

Visualizing the Supported Deities

This has two parts:

1. Visualizing the Principal [Deity]
2. Visualizing the Retinue

Visualizing the Principal [Deity]

This has two parts:

1. Visualizing the Principal Father
2. Visualizing the Principal Mother

Visualizing the Principal Father

From the root tantra,

> In the center of that is a lotus
> With petals and a blazing navel and corolla.
> The Hero arranged in the center
> Can terrify even Bhairava.
> He is splendorously ablaze,
> With the great laughter of HA HA.
>
> He is adorned with a rosary of human heads,
> Has three excellent eyes and four powerful faces,
> Is gracefully wearing an elephant skin,
> And has good eyebrows separated by a vajra.
> The hands hold a katvanga and a human skull,
> And he is gracefully adorned with a rosary of fifty [heads].

Recite, "[Upon this lotus] I arise as the bhagawan Heruka . . ." and so forth. The translation equivalent of *bhagawan* is "destroyer, endowed, and [transcended]." "Destroy" means to engage in the destruction of the two obstructions, attachment, the four maras, and so forth. "Endowed" refers to power, a good body, glory, fame, exalted wisdom, perseverance, and all things excellent, which are called "the six good fortunes"; thus this is being endowed with the six fortunes. Although "transcend" is not part of the Sanskrit, it was added by the Tibetan translators to clarify the meaning. Thus "destroy and endowed" refer to the worldly deity Ishvara and so forth, or it refers to [Heruka] engaging and becoming superior to him, hence it says "transcend." The translation equivalent of "glorious" [as in glorious Heruka], is *Shri* [in Sanskrit]. HE is the selflessness of persons; RU is the wisdom of emptiness [realizing] the selflessness of phenomena; and KA is the method of great bliss, which symbolizes bliss and emptiness.

[Heruka's] body is magnificent like a mountain of sapphire. As for his four faces, the principal face is dark like a rain cloud, his left face is green like an emerald, his rear face is red like coral, and his right face is yellow like gold. At the center of the faces is one neck, with the ears very close to each other, similar to a statue cast in relief. Each face has three long and narrow eyes. Concerning the twelve arms, although they are the nature of light, without bones and so forth, when looking at them from the outside, there would be six arms on both the right and left sides coming out of one shoulder as though coming from the mouth of one cup. On the forehead is the hero's silk ribbon. Above that are skulls adorned with a rosary of five-pronged vajras. [Heruka's] body is neither too fat nor too thin, but is very muscular and adorned with the clothing of a sage. His left leg is bent and his right leg is outstretched; from the tips of the toes of one foot to the other is five hand-spans. His right leg [treads] on black Bhairava who has four hands; the first two are pressed together and the lower two hold a damaru and a sword, with [Bhairava's] head turned to the right while [Heruka] is pressing down on his left ear. His left leg [treads] on red Kalarati who has four hands. Her first two are pressed together, and the other two hold a skull cup and a katvanga; lying on her back, Heruka presses down upon her breasts.

Of the primary hands—that is, the first[57]—the right hand holds a golden five-pronged vajra, and the left holds a bell with a five-pronged vajra handle and is embracing the Mother just below the breasts. The next two [hands] hold the body of a flayed elephant skin of Ganesh, with its head to the right and its hairy side facing outward. [Heruka's] two hands are outstretched, making a threatening mudra with the tips of the

---

57. When looking at a painting of Heruka, it is not obvious which are the first hands, which are the second hands, and so forth. When referring to the order of the hands, it depends on the order that they come out of the shoulder. The first two hold the vajra and bell and embrace the Mother; the next two hold the elephant skin at his back; the third right hand holds a damaru; the fourth an axe; the fifth a curved knife; and the sixth holds a three-pointed spear. His third right hand holds a katvanga; the fourth a skull cup; the fifth a vajra noose; and the sixth a four-faced head of Brahma.

fingers level with his eyes and holding the hind and forelegs on the left side [of Ganesh's body so that his head faces toward the right of Heruka]. The third right hand holds a damaru made of skull. The fourth holds an axelike [weapon] marked with a half vajra at its tip. In the fifth [hand] is a curved knife, twelve finger-widths long. In the sixth is a short spear with a handle and three points. In the third left hand is a katvanga with a five-pronged vajra at its tip.[58] Below that [five-pronged vajra on the katvanga], symbolizing the body, speech, and mind, are three human heads: a white dry head, a red old head, and a moist black head. Below that, symbolizing the four enlightened actions, is a variegated vajra. Below that is a vase filled with bodhichitta nectar, a small golden bell, and a hanging three-pointed pendant. Below that is the eight-sided handle [staff], its lower tip being a single-pointed vajra. It is said that you must hold the katvanga so it is tucked inward into the armpit touching the breast ornament.[59]

In the fourth [hand] is a skull cup filled with blood. In the fifth is a black noose marked with a half-vajra tip. In the sixth is the yellow head of Brahma with four faces. On the crown of Heruka's head is a bone wheel with eight spokes, in the center of which is a nine-faceted jewel, and at the tip is a five-pronged vajra; these are two aspects of a life tree. His black hair is tied up; the lower crest [of hair] is bound by two ribbons above and below, above which its upper crest is marked with a vajra jewel. On the front side of the topknot is a variegated vajra. On the left side above that, it is marked with a half moon. On each head there are two rosaries of black vajras strung together above and below. There are five dried skulls, which are the nature of the five tathagatas, and all five tips are endowed with five jewels. Hanging from the mouths of the dried skulls are nets of full and half length, and the lower ends come down reaching just to the center of the eyes.

58. Everything listed in the rest of the paragraph represents the qualities of the katvanga held in the third left hand.
59. The chest ornament is worn by Brahmins while making offerings.

[The Nine Moods]

By parting his lips slightly his facial expressions change. Revealing his four bared fangs is the "terrifying" mood.[60]

The body standing in a prideful manner represents the "haughtiness" mood. Suppressing Bhairava and Kalarati with his feet is the "heroic" mood. The wrinkles of wrath at his forehead represent the "repulsive" mood. These are the three physical moods.

His face in a smiling aspect is the "laughing" mood. The four fangs bared is the "wrathful" mood. The tongue rolled up is the "terrifying" mood. These are the three verbal moods.

His long and narrow eyes represent the "compassionate" mood. His eyes wide open is the "wondrous" mood. Looking from the corner of the eyes at the Mother represents the "peaceful" mood. These are the three mental moods, making nine moods in all.

He has a lower garment of a tiger skin. When embracing the Mother, her skull cup must be revealed to the back face of [Heruka] with her left hand. The fifty moist human heads strung together with intestines as a necklace hang down from the neck to the thighs. The bone earrings are round and are marked with a three-pronged vajra. At the lower tips are three nets of bone and two half nets, adorned by five in all. The necklace is at the front and center of the throat and has sixteen pieces of vajra bone. At both the right and the left side are strings of bone going through each side, and from each one eight strands of bone hang down, forming a crisscross pattern. The chest ornament is directly in front of the center of the chest. The front has eight bone vajras and the back is indefinite. From that the two bone rosaries are aligned so that one goes over the left shoulder and under the right arm, and one goes over the right shoulder and under the left arm. The lower ends of the strands connect the front with the back.

From the tips of the vajra pieces come full and half-length garlands. There are bracelets and anklets on the hands and the feet. Directly in front of the two shoulders are three bone vajras between, with a rosary of five each that cross each other and are tied together. The lower part is

---

60. This is one of the moods of speech listed below.

beautified with full and half-length strands hanging down together with small bells. The skirt is in front of the navel, and in the center there are sixty-four vajra pieces. To the right and left there are five bone rosaries with no spokes between each. These sixteen form a crisscross pattern from which bones hang down in five nets and thirteen half-nets. All of these eighteen have *sharpu* hanging at their ends as well as small bells and jeweled drumstick handles hanging down, reaching the level of the knees. The bone above the center of Heruka's head symbolizes your own channel petals with the three tips of the vajra hanging down in strands. The square chest ornament at his heart has a circle inside, and there are rosaries of two, four, and eight, all symbolizing power. Heruka's entire body is smeared with ashes of human bone.

Thus meditate on the meaning and purity of the symbolism as follows: Heruka's dark blue body symbolizes the unchanging [nature] of the dharmadhatu. The four faces symbolize the four doors to liberation: emptiness, signlessness, wishlessness, and noncomposition. Suppressing the wrathful male and female deities under his feet symbolizes abandoning the two extremes: the extreme of permanence as an existent samsara and the extreme of annihilation as a nonexistent nirvana. Holding the vajra and bell in two hands embracing the Mother symbolizes the inseparable union of bliss and emptiness. The damaru, axe, curved knife, and three-pointed spear symbolize respectively the sound of arousing supreme joy in the buddhas, cutting through the faults of the three doors, cutting through the conceptions grasping at extremes, and piercing through the delusions of the three realms. The katvanga and skull cup symbolize inducing the simultaneously born great bliss through melting the bodhichitta. The noose symbolizes binding one's own and others' mental continua through great bliss. The four-faced Brahma head symbolizes actualizing the nonabiding nirvana. The hair tied up in a topknot symbolizes that virtues are ever increasing. The variegated vajra symbolizes engaging in four enlightened actions for the welfare of sentient beings. The rosary of black vajras [at the forehead] interwoven with the five dried skulls as a crown ornament symbolizes the arising of the illusory body from the clear light. The half moon [on the crown] symbolizes that the bliss of bodhichitta abides in the channel wheel at the crown. The changing faces symbolize reversing all of your wrong views to abiding in the correct view. The four bared fangs symbolize destroying the four maras [demons].[61] The appearance of the nine moods and so forth are the nature of the five [buddha] families such as Vairochana and so forth and symbolize the five aspects of tranquil, abiding concentration. Chenma[62] and so forth symbolize the four aspects of the wisdom of superior seeing, which are the nature of the four mothers. The tiger-skin loin cloth symbolizes purifying the delusions such as attachment and so forth. The necklace of fifty human heads is the nature of the Sanskrit vowels and consonants and symbolizes the virtue of both method and wisdom. The six mudras symbolize the six perfections. The ash of human bone [smeared on the body] symbolizes melting the bodhichitta that pervades the inside of all the channels, thereby inducing simultaneously born [great bliss.] Thus, by recalling the symbolic meaning of the purities [of Heruka's body] and meditating on it, you ripen your virtuous roots to generate in your mental continuum during the path of the second stage [the completion stage]. In this way you establish the unique potentiality to manifest the aspect of the resultant-time body of Heruka.

Visualizing the Principal Mother

Recite, "As the bhagawan [I am embracing the bhagawati . . .]" and so forth. The *Root Tantra* states,

> In front of glorious Heruka
> Arrange the goddess Vajravarahi
> —the most terrifying goddess—
> With three eyes and a wrathful form.
>
> Her skull cup is filled with intestines, and
> From her mouth blood drips out.
> With a mudra in all directions, she threatens
> Gods, demigods, as well as humans.

---

61. The four maras or demons are death, the aggregates, delusions, and the actual demon called "the son of the gods."
62. Chenma is Tibetan for Lochana, the consort of Buddha Vairochana.

Thus, she is facing the bhagawan in embrace. The meaning of *bhagawati* is similar to the meaning of [*bhagawan* for the] Father. *Vajra* is "method" and means to engage the nondifferentiated [nature] of great bliss and the wisdom of emptiness. *Varahi* destroys the form of ignorance and symbolizes the mirrorlike exalted wisdom lineage of Vairochana. Her body is red like coral. Her three eyes are wide open and prominent. From her widespread *bhaga*,[63] blood drips out, and she is in an extremely passionate mood. Having abandoned grasping at the signs [of inherent existence], she is naked, with her hair hanging loose. Symbolizing the union of the conventional illusory body and the ultimate clear light being inseparably unified in one taste, her skull cup in her left hand, filled with the blood of the four maras and so forth, is offered to the back face of the Father. Symbolizing the exalted wisdom of bliss and emptiness having annihilated the two obstructions from the root, the curved knife in her right hand threatens [evil beings] with a wrathful mudra. Symbolizing the blazing of *chandali* [inner heat], she blazes like a fire at the end of an eon. Her two calves wrap around the Father just above his thighs and are perfectly entwined. She is the nature of compassion and bestows simultaneously born great bliss.

Except for the ash, the Mother has the same mudras [as the Father]. The ash symbolizes the perfection of wisdom, and since the Mother herself is the aspect of wisdom[, the ash is not needed]. The other five mudras represent the other five perfections. Her head is adorned with dried skulls and bone ornaments like the Father. The necklace of fifty dried human heads symbolizes that the Mother is on the side of the wisdom of emptiness, and her body is endowed with the method of great bliss. Hence, imagine that the Father and Mother are both standing amid a blazing fire and are endowed with an aura that outshines all worlds. It is taught that one should meditate [on oneself as Heruka Father and Mother in this way] with clear appearance and divine pride.

Visualizing the Retinue

This has two parts:

1. Visualizing the Four Goddesses in the Directions

63. *Bhaga* is Sanskrit for "vagina" and is used interchangeably with the word "lotus."

2. Visualizing the Vases and Skull Cups in the Intermediate Directions

Visualizing the Four Goddesses in the Directions

Recite, "On the petals of the lotus…" and so forth. The four goddesses Chenma and so forth are displayed in the aspect of the four goddesses—Dakini and so forth; in this way they should be displayed. Previously, for the sake of bestowing the common and supreme attainments upon practitioners, they subdued the four wrathful consorts [of Bhairava]. Furthermore, on the eastern petal of the variegated lotus is Dakini who is dark like a rain cloud. On the northern petal is Lama, which means "Beautiful Goddess," and who is green like an emerald. On the western petal is Kandharohi, which means "Portion-Born Goddess," and who is red like coral. On the southern petal is Rupini, who is yellow like gold. All four have one face, three eyes, and bared fangs with a slightly laughing expression. They are naked with their hair hanging loose. Of their four hands, the first right hand holds a curved knife, and the left holds a skull cup in the manner of embrace at the level of their heart. The lower right hand holds a damaru, and the lower left hand holds a katvanga in the crook of their elbow. They stand with their right legs outstretched. They are adorned with the five mudras and so forth that are said to be the same as those of the Principal Mother.

In the texts it is taught that there is a lotus petal as a cushion for the four goddesses of the retinue. Many other sadhanas don't describe any more than that. Yet the sadhana of the five deities by the supreme conqueror [the Seventh Dalai Lama] Kelsang Gyatso, entitled *The Powerful Conqueror of Great Bliss*, and so forth, as well as the mandala ritual usually teach that there is both a sun and a corpse seat. Therefore, unless one is explaining the action deity, in which case there is merely a sun seat, if you check, you will find that it is not correct [to have the sun seat but no corpse seat].

Visualizing the Vases and Skull Cups in the Intermediate Directions

Recite, "In the intermediate directions…" and so forth. Upon the four petals of the intermediate directions are moon seats and red vases in the shape of victory vases filled with white nectar. Upon these are skull cups, in one piece, with the foreheads facing inward and filled with red nectar, which symbolize method and wisdom.

Meditating on the Corresponding Purity

This has three parts:

1. Blessing the Four Places
2. From Blessing the Secret Place to Inducing the Four Joys
3. The Actual Meditation on the Purity

Blessing the Four Places

Recite, "At the Father's navel . . ." and so forth. At the Father's navel and heart on moon cushions are the Mother's essence mantra. At the Mother's throat and crown on moon cushions are the Mother's close-essence mantra. At the Mother's navel and heart are the sun cushions with the Father's essence mantra. At the Father's throat and crown are sun cushions with the close-essence mantra of the Father.[64] At these places, directly in front of the four chakras, or channel wheels, and facing outward are sun or moon mandalas as if they were mirrors standing upright reflecting the form of the mantra rosaries on the surface. They are red in color and arranged counterclockwise, and, when you enter into embrace, red light rays radiate while mixing, embracing, kissing, and so forth.

From Blessing the Secret Place to Inducing the Four Joys

Although it is not taught in the scriptures, you should recite, "From the secret place of the Father . . ." and so forth. Furthermore, imagine the secret place of the Father melts into light into unobservable [emptiness] and thus cleanses ordinary appearance and conception [of the secret place]. From that comes a white letter HUM, which melts into light

---

64. This presentation is slightly different from that given in the sadhana.

and transforms externally into the shape of a vajra sign [that is, penis] and internally is in the aspect of a white five-pronged vajra. It is, for example, like placing one's own vajra in a leather pouch and blocking the hole that opens at the central prong. Suddenly, at its tip is a red letter BHYA that melts into light from which arises a red jewel. Inside the hole comes a yellow BHYA with its head pointing inward but not showing from the outside. Imagine that thick yellow light rays radiate and block [the hole of the vajra] so that there are not any intervening spaces.

Furthermore, the white vajra at the secret place of the Father symbolizes that it is filled with white bodhichitta. The five tips symbolize the five inner channels. The red jewel symbolizes that the white bodhichitta is mixed with a little red [bodhichitta]. The yellow BHYA blocking [the hole of the vajra] symbolizes the blockage of the emission of bodhichitta by arresting [the flow of] the downward-voiding wind.

Similarly imagine that the secret place of the Mother also becomes unobservable and transforms into a red AH, which melts into light, and the outer aspect transforms into a bhaga, and the inner into a three-petaled lotus with a hole in the center. In the center of that there suddenly emerges a white letter DHYA, from which comes a white stamen together with anthers. Imagine that inside the hole comes a yellow DHYA with its head facing inward, radiating light rays that block [the hole]. The red lotus at the secret place of the Mother symbolizes that it is filled with drops of red bodhichitta. The three petals of the lotus symbolize that inside there are three primary channels at the lower tip. The white stamen symbolizes that the red bodhichitta possesses a little white bodhichitta. The yellow letter DHYA symbolizes the downward-voiding wind as [explained] earlier.

Next, bless the four places and the secret place with OM AH HUM. The Father and Mother embrace each other; they are kissing, frolicking, and so forth. At that time the wind comes forth from the lotus of the Mother like smoke, rises, and enters into the Father's vajra. The fire at his navel blazes and melts the bodhichitta at the crown, which descends through the path of the central channel. Recite, "When it arrives at the throat, there is joy . . ." and so forth, whereby the four joys are generated at the four places. Finally, when the bodhichitta arrives at the tip of the jewel, it is arrested by the letter BHYA and held there from being emitted. Imagine that your mind becomes the nonconceptual concentration of great bliss and simultaneously produce an experience of bliss. At this time recall the view of emptiness and sustain the union of inseparable bliss and emptiness. Then, generate the powerful conviction that the entire supporting and supported mandalas are also the nature of inseparable bliss and emptiness. At this point, when entering into embrace, as joy arises in dependence upon undertaking the visualizations, slowly, and with conviction, enter into the union of bliss and emptiness all the way up to the final, fourth joy, and then remain with that for a long time. All the parts of the ritual that follow, such as meditation on the deity, mantra recitation, and so forth, must all be done while generating this [yoga of bliss and emptiness.] Thus, this practice becomes a sacred method for ripening one's mental continuum for generating the realizations of the completion stage, a practice described as "the principal yoga of generation stage."

The Actual Meditation on the Purity

Thus, from the visualizations of entering into embrace and so forth, one generates bliss; this very union of inseparable bliss and emptiness is the nature of the thirty-seven aspects of enlightenment, which are the following:

1. The close placement of mindfulness of body
2. The close placement of mindfulness of feelings
3. The close placement of mindfulness of phenomena
4. The close placement of mindfulness of mind

These are the four close placements of mindfulness.

5. The legs of the miracle powers of aspiration
6. The legs of the miracle powers of effort
7. The legs of the miracle powers of mind
8. The legs of the miracle powers of analysis

These are the four legs of the miracle powers.

  9. The power of faith
10. The power of effort
11. The power of mindfulness
12. The power of concentration
13. The power of wisdom

These are the five powers.

14. The force of wisdom and the five sense powers
15. The force of faith
16. The force of effort
17. The force of mindfulness
18. The force of concentration

These are the five forces of wisdom and five sense powers.

19. The branches of enlightenment of concentration
20. The branch of enlightenment of effort
21. The branch of enlightenment of joy
22. The branch of enlightenment of correct suppleness
23. The branch of enlightenment of correct discernment of phenomena
24. The branch of mindfulness of enlightenment
25. The branch of equanimity of enlightenment

These are the seven branches of enlightenment.

26. Correct view
27. Correct conception
28. [Correct speech]
29. Correct end of actions
30. Correct livelihood
31. Correct effort
32. Correct mindfulness
33. Correct concentration

These are the eight correct branches of the paths of a superior being.

34. Generating virtuous dharmas not yet generated
35. Protecting those [virtues] already generated
36. Abandoning nonvirtuous dharmas already generated
37. Not generating those [nonvirtues] not yet generated

These are the four correct abandonments.

As these arise in the aspect of the five deities, think that the deities appear but have no inherent existence and as such should be viewed like an image appearing in a mirror. This is the primary meaning. Beginners should recall the view of inseparable bliss and emptiness and develop conviction that each deity has such a nature. This is the primary meaning of meditating on the thirty-seven aspects of enlightenment.

Now, concerning how you should meditate. The thirty-seven aspects of enlightenment symbolize that the principal trainees of this path need to be well acquainted with all the paths of the three vehicles. From the perspective of its ultimate function, this path of inseparable bliss and emptiness is the essence of the three vehicles. Determine that you are establishing the potential to accomplish the final resultant-time exalted wisdom of Heruka as a single entity appearing in the aspect of the five deities whose body and mind are one nature.

Wearing the Armor and the Entering of the Wisdom Beings

This has two parts:

1. Wearing the Armor
2. Entering of the Wisdom Beings

Wearing the Armor

At this point in Je [Rinpoche's text entitled] *Wish Fulfilling*, each pair of the [armor deities] is generated complete with arms and faces on both the Father and Mother. Also the armor of the Father is together with the Mother, and the armor of the Mother is a solitary female [armor deity]. It is also said that the armor of both the Father and Mother have solitary Father and Mother [armor deities]. Thus, both explanations were also given by Luipa and Ghantapa according to both their commentaries. According to the intention of both of their commentaries to the sadhana, they also say that both have solitary Father and Mother armor deities. Here, from the perspective of the abbreviated sadhana, instead of having Vajrasattva and so forth at their individual places, the places are merely marked by the mantras OM HA and so forth in the nature [of the armor deities]. To make it still more abbreviated, you can merely mark the three places with the three seed syllables [OM AH HUM], which is said to be permissible to begin with.

Recite, "At my heart…" and so forth. Visualize that at your heart, inside your skin but outside of your flesh, [between the skin and the muscle,] on a moon support, in the nature of Vajrasattva, is a white OM HA, surrounded by white light, like a form reflected in a mirror. In this way apply the same reasoning to the others—that is, at your head, at the hair line, the crown of the head, the two shoulders, at the two eyes, and so forth. The throat is said to be directly in front of the Adam's apple.[65]

Then, at the crown of the deities on a moon seat, in the nature of the vajra body, is a white OM. At their throats upon a lotus, in the nature of the vajra speech, is a red AH. At their hearts upon a sun, in the nature of vajra mind, is a blue HUM. It is also permissible to [merely] generate the seed syllables of the body, speech, and mind. Thus, through this meditation, you protect your concentrative meditation on deity yoga from any distraction by obstructing spirits and so forth. Through this your mind remains unmoving with stable concentration on deity yoga, and you are protected from the obstacles of obstructing spirits and so forth. Moreover, it is said that you also need this to accomplish the common and uncommon attainments.

---

65. This probably refers to the armor deity at the throat of the Mother.

Entering of the Wisdom Beings

Recite, "PHAIM, light rays [radiate from the letter HUM]..." and so forth. Release your legs from the vajra position and place the big toe of your outstretched right foot upon the big toe of your left foot. Join your two hands so that the two middle fingers touch and the index fingers are held inside the circle created by your thumb and index fingers, and then extend the other fingers. This is the blazing mudra, which should be held at the center of your forehead. With your eyes turned a little downward, bring the look upward from the left, and make the first circle counterclockwise and then clockwise, and recite PHAIM with a wrathful evocation. Simultaneously from the HUM at the heart of all the deities, countless red hooklike light rays radiate to the ten directions and invoke the heroes, heroines, and powerful goddesses who abide in limitless worldly realms. These empowering deities become the wheel of exalted wisdom in the aspect of the mandala of sixty-two deities of the mandala of Chakrasamvara. Goddesses holding outer offering substances such as flowers and so forth, many beautiful goddesses skilled in the complete arts of love in graceful stances and so forth, as well as goddesses for making the secret offering, holding outer offering substances such as flowers and so forth, are invoked with inconceivable numbers of [deities] to the space before you, thereby completely filling the realms of space. The light rays then dissolve back into your heart. Your four faces proclaim the Kandharohi mantra with a wrathful sound. Imagine that simultaneously a limitless number of Kandharohi goddesses emanate out to dispel those obstructing spirits that follow after the wisdom beings.

Recite, OM AHRGHAM PRATITZA AH HUM.... At that time imagine that limitless white water offering goddesses emanate and make offerings to the wisdom beings. When you recite DZA, imagine that the wisdom beings are summoned and come to rest just above the commitment beings, like one person stacked upon another. Recite HUM and imagine that the wisdom beings dissolve into the commitment beings and arise like a form reflected in a mirror or like milk and water that don't [quite] mix; in this same way the wisdom beings and the commitment beings don't [quite] mix. Recite BAM and think that just like water poured into water the wisdom beings and the commitment beings mix inseparably. Recite HO and, like the desire for a lustful maiden, imagine that the wisdom beings enter the commitment beings and become nondual. Furthermore, you must dissolve the Principal and retinue, up to the supporting mandala, the rosary of light, the charnel grounds, and so forth.

The reason you must do this is to stop adhering to the belief that you and the wisdom beings are separate. It also functions to stabilize the divine pride of being inseparable in nature from the wisdom beings. As the commitment beings are endowed with power, because you as the yogi are acting as the commitment being, the wisdom beings will bless your aggregates, elements, and sources, and you will become the resultant refuge by quickly attaining [the state] of Chakrasamvara.

Then recite OM YOGA SHUDDHA ... and so forth, and contemplate that the suchness of all phenomena and the exalted wisdom of great bliss are inseparable in nature. Such is the definitive meaning of Heruka. Imagine that this arises in the aspect of the interpretive Heruka with faces and hands and the supporting and supported mandalas. Moreover, it is taught that you must imagine that the Principal Father and Mother are part of this exalted wisdom and hence the basis of imputation for the conception "I," thereby establishing divine pride.

From Bestowing Empowerment up to Sealing

This has two parts:

1. Bestowing Empowerment
2. Sealing with the Lord of the Lineage

Bestowing Empowerment

Recite OM AHRGHAM ... and so forth. The offering goddesses make water offerings to the empowering deities as before. To the empowering goddesses, Heruka Chakrasamvara, and so forth, recite, "All the tathagatas bestow empowerment directly." By requesting in this way, the eight goddesses of the commitment wheel dispel interfering spirits; the twenty-four heroes of the three wheels recite auspicious verses [such as]

"That which definitely emerges from the dharmadhatu . . ." among others. The twenty-four heroines recite,

> The subject matter is the vajra emptiness
> Because it is indestructible and unbreakable.
> It is solid and with essence, not insubstantial,
> Not burnt, and uncut.

Thus, the principal subject matter of *Vajra Peak Tantra* is the teachings on emptiness, which is revealed with this vajra song. The reason for the vajra proclamation is to [teach] emptiness. For example, a diamond is also an entity such that it cannot be burnt or cut and one is unable to break or split it. It is taught that because emptiness is also like this it is called "vajra."

With vases and skull cups from the intermediate directions, the four goddesses are the nature of Rupavajra goddesses and so forth. Therefore, they go out holding offering substances of the desire objects and make offerings to you. The Principal decides to give the empowerment and directs the four mothers together with Varahi to hold aloft five jeweled vases filled with nectar. As you recite the mantra, the water descends and bestows empowerment upon all the deities.

The meaning of the mantra is this: OM is the forerunner of the mantra. SARWA means "all." TATHA means "thus." GATA means "gone." ABHI means "directly." SHEKATA means "bestow empowerment." SAMAYA means "commitment." SHRIYE is for the sake of [making one] glorious.

In that way a stream of nectar water descends and bestows empowerment through the crown of your head. The stream of nectar enters the Brahmin aperture. It is said that you should imagine that your body as the Father and Mother and the bodies of the four goddesses are filled up with nectar from below, and extraordinary exalted wisdom of bliss and emptiness is generated in your mental continuum.

SEALING WITH THE LORD OF THE LINEAGE

Recite, "The Principal is [adorned by Vajrasattva] . . ." and so forth. The excess water overflows onto the crown of their heads and completely transforms. Upon the center of the nine-faceted jewel on the crown of the head of the Father is Vajrasattva; on the Mother, Akshobya; and on the four dakinis, Ratnasambhava, who together become their crown ornaments and are the lords of the lineage. Their colors and hand implements are in accordance with the empowerment ritual, entitled *Essence of Great Bliss.* This establishes the power to accomplish the five exalted wisdoms and, as the outer generation stage, is related to the vase empowerment. At this point it is not taught that one should bestow more than just the water empowerment on oneself as the deity. In Atisha's commentary, there is an excellent teaching explaining that one should receive the four empowerments. Mahasiddha Tso Kye[66] also says in his Hevajra commentary that all four empowerments should be bestowed. Therefore, imagine that the four heart yoginis of the deity dissolve into Varahi who enters into embrace with Heruka. Next, they bestow the bodhichitta [from the joined organs of the Father and Mother] and place it on your tongue, and you imagine you generate the exalted wisdom of great bliss.[67] This is related to "blessing the self"[68] of the illusory body and is related to the secret empowerment. Next, imagine the Mother dissolves into the consort appearing as the consort Varahi for you as Heruka. Imagine you enter into embrace and, due to the winds dissolving into [the central channel], you generate the simultaneously born bliss. This is the ultimate truth of the clear light and is related to the wisdom empowerment. Then Heruka says, "Child of the lineage, in dependence upon uniting with a consort..." and continues up to "Through this explanation, imagine that you generate an understanding of union." This union is related to the fourth empowerment.

Whether you are doing merely the water empowerment and sealing with the lord of the lineage or subsequently receiving the remaining [three of the] four empowerments, at this point you should dissolve the empowering deities into yourself. Thus, through the bestowal of the empowerment, obstructing spirits, obscurations, and the [motivations of the] lower vehicle are dispelled. You become a suitable vessel for meditation and recitation and for accomplishing the actions of pacifying and

66. Tib. *mThso skyes.*
67. At this point you can taste the inner offering and imagine it is the secret substance.
68. This is not the same "blessing the self" that is the first of the five stages of the completion stage of Ghantapa, but instead is a reference to the illusory body, using language borrowed from the Guhyasamaja tantra.

so forth, restoring degenerated bodhichitta as well as degenerated vows and commitments. It also establishes imprints so that in the future you will receive an empowerment from a buddha and will accomplish the resultant-time *ushnisha* by having your crown sealed with the lord of the lineage.

From Making Offerings and Praises up to Meditating on the Mandala

This has three parts:

1. Making Offerings
2. Making Praises
3. Meditating on the Mandala

Making Offerings

This has five parts:

1. Making Outer Offerings
2. Inner Offering
3. The Secret and Suchness Offerings
4. Offering the Mantras
5. Offering Praise

Making Outer Offerings

Recite the offering [mantras] and so forth. You can understand the merit field from the previous explanation. Apply the same reasoning to the offering goddesses being emanated and withdrawn and so forth. The offering goddesses have peaceful gazes, wear strands of pearls, have voluptuous breasts with narrow cleavage, and their clothes are a little loose, revealing their beautiful lower bodies. Their waists are very thin, and they have broad stomachs that swirl to the right. The lower part of their bodies and their vaginas are thick. They move with ease and grace, have smiling faces, and gaze with desirous eyes. Moreover, they must be meditated upon as having arisen from the state of perfect concentration and so forth. In that way they are in the aspect of goddesses holding an inconceivable number of offering substances. Thus emanated from the seed syllable at your heart, imagine that, through making these offerings, the Principal and retinue all generate the uncontaminated, extraordinary, exalted wisdom of great bliss in their mental continua. This is related to the outer vase empowerment and the path of the generation stage.

Although the Sakyapas [assert] that, for the self-generation, concentration is of supreme importance, and for the front-generation, the offering is of supreme importance, for them making offerings at this point is not considered to be very important. The foremost great being [Lama Tsongkhapa] himself has instead said, "It is an extremely important quintessential instruction to make offerings [to oneself] now at the time of the path in accordance with the inner division of the resultant four complete purities offered in accordance with the aspect of complete purity of enjoyment at the time of the result."

Inner Offering

Recite, "[To the mouth] of my kind root…" and so forth. Imagine a limitless number of rasa-vajra goddesses emanate, holding skull cups of inner offering vessels from which nectar is poured out and offered to the tongues of the guests as a three-pronged vajra from which tubes of light partake of all the essence of the [inner offering]. With the thumb of your left hand symbolizing the Mother's lotus, and the ring finger symbolizing the Father's vajra, imagine from the point of their churning, bodhichitta nectar descends and is offered [to the guests]. Sprinkle [the inner offering] from the level of your eyebrows; make the inner offering with OM AH HUM to your kind root guru and lineage gurus who surround him counterclockwise. They sit upon a moon seat at the heart of the lord of the lineage who is in the center of the nine-faceted jewel as the head ornament of the Principal [Heruka].

Recite the essence and close-essence mantras of the Father and Mother, attach the three letters [OM AH HUM], and sprinkle from the level of your heart. Attach the three syllables to the mantras of the four goddesses and sprinkle according to the direction [of each of the four goddesses].

Visualize that at your heart is yourself as the deity, at your throat is your root guru as the deity, and at your crown are the lineage gurus as the deity; to these three offer [the inner offering] by touching your heart, throat, and crown [respectively]. The dharma protectors are inside the eastern door facing inward; [to them offer the inner offering] from the level of the navel. The heroes and yoginis are dwelling in the charnel grounds. Also abiding in the charnel grounds are the directional protectors, field protectors, nagas, and so forth; to them offer [the inner offering] from the level of the secret place. Beyond the charnel grounds are the landlords abiding in their natural abodes and all sentient beings transformed into the aspect of Heruka; to them offer [the inner offering] from the level of the knees. Offer [the inner offering] together with the mudra of supreme giving, and imagine all the guests are delighted by the uncontaminated bliss. This offering is related to the secret empowerment and the path of the illusory body.

THE SECRET AND SUCHNESS OFFERINGS

Recite, "The Father and Mother enter into embrace..." and so forth. Imagine that the Father and Mother enter into embrace and generate the four joys as done earlier, and the Principal and all of his retinue experience simultaneously born great bliss. This is the secret offering and is related to the wisdom-exalted-wisdom empowerment and the path of the clear light. Imagine that, in dependence upon this, the Principal and all of his retinue generate simultaneously born bliss in their mental continua, which multiplies, and through this, they realize emptiness, which becomes the exalted wisdom of inseparable bliss and emptiness. Meditate on this for a long time. This is the suchness offering and is related to the word empowerment.

From among all the offerings, the supreme is the secret and suchness offering; therefore, you should distinguish these two visualizations very well and meditate on them for a long time. This is the great quintessential instruction of Je Rinpoche who says, "It has been said on many occasions that all the offerings arise as the display of inseparable bliss and emptiness; this is the sacred method by which you easily complete your training in the accumulations [of merit and wisdom], and it has been taught that these are of utmost importance."

Offering the Mantras

Next, recite [the mantras from the sadhana] and so forth. Imagine that the offering goddesses, in aspect as before, touch the feet of the deities of the mandala and then make praises [with the mantras]. At [the same time] hold your hands in prayer at your heart, and as you recite the individual mantras, you should visualize clearly each of the deities' bodies and recite all the mantras of the Principal and retinue. At that time visualize clearly that the deities [generate] in their mental continua the definitive meaning of mantra—the exalted wisdom of inseparable bliss and emptiness. Visualizing that this occurs in the mind is the uncommon meaning of offering the mantra of this tantra.

Offering Praise

To elaborate, recite the [mantras] as a praise. To elaborate further recite the two sets of eight lines of praise together with the praise [in verse]. If you wish to make it shorter, it is permissible to merely recite the two verses, "O Great and Glorious Heruka..." and so forth. Here I will just explain their meaning.

"Glorious Heruka" is the nature of the inseparable exalted wisdom of bliss and emptiness. The "great hero" is the one who destroys all inner demons—the two obstructions and so forth, and the outer [demons]— the deity Maha Ishvara and so forth. As the nature of the exalted wisdom undefiled by stains, he is "pure." He is undivided by the elaborations of the two appearances, therefore he is "vajra." The exalted wisdom controls desire, therefore his is the "principal powerful lord." Through embracing and kissing, passion is generated and so forth. Thereby the Principal himself generates great desire and simultaneously born great bliss in his mental continuum together with the Mother. [Therefore], "I respectfully prostrate to Vajravarahi."

Recite, "Respectfully I prostrate[69] to the heroes, heroines, and powerful goddesses and the entire collection of deities of the mandala who abide in the places and near-places, the tsandohas and near-tsandohas...," also

---

69. This comes at the end of the verse in English.

called "obtaining aspirations," "...the meeting places and close-meeting places and the charnel grounds and close-charnel grounds."

In the *Root Tantra* it says,

> And then, further explanation of
> The grounds and abodes of the yoginis:
> The limbs of Heruka's body are
> The nature of all things stable and moving.
>
> The seat is the "Very Joyous" ground;
> Likewise the adjacent seat is "Stainless."
> This field is "Illuminating,"
> The close-place is "Radiant,"
> Tsandoha is "Manifest,"
> The close-tsandoha is "Difficult to Overcome,"
> The gathering is "Gone Afar,"
> The close-gathering is "Unshakable,"
> The charnel ground is "Good Intelligence," and
> The close-charnel ground is the "Cloud of Dharma."[70]
>
> Through the teaching and practice of Shri Heruka,
> The grounds abide within oneself.
> The grounds of the ten perfections are in
> The symbolic language of the yogini.

As is expressed [in the above verses], the places are related to the spiritual grounds of a bodhisattva, and the heroes and heroines abiding in those places are equated with realizations.

Meditating on the Mandala

Recite, "At this point..." and so forth. If you are receiving a full-fledged practical commentary on the generation stage by a skilled guru who

---

70. This is the relationship of the ten bodhisattva grounds with ten places, with the fifth and six reversed from their usual order.

explains it from his own experience, you should come to know the perfect method for generating the uncommon concentration of the gross and subtle generation stage of this tradition. You, as the disciple, while receiving instructions from your guru concerning the methods for enhancing your experience, should strive to dispel obstacles.

As beginners we should have a proper way to meditate. Therefore, we must train in the visualizations from the instantaneous self-generation up to this point, which serves as the foundation. Also, we should think that this is like the ripening agent for the roots of virtue for the completion stage, and, if we have this powerful intention, we will not be distracted by other visualizations and will eliminate mental sinking and excitement. In this way we should continuously meditate.

As an antidote to ordinary conceptions, meditate on the celestial mansion and deity with the thought that you are in a buddha's pure land in the actual body of a buddha, and meditate on that pure thought with powerful divine pride. As the antidote to ordinary appearances, visualize each of the unique features of the supporting and supported [mandalas]. If earlier [in the sadhana] it was not clear, later on you will not be able to meditate. Then when you are able to meditate without forgetting what came earlier, you should practice scanning meditation with strong faith while slowly reciting the words of the ritual.

When reaching this point, visualize clearly from the charnel grounds up to the Principal, and from the Principal back to the charnel grounds. Visualize these two, alternating until they are established as a unified thought of single-pointed [concentration]. Those with more developed minds may have clear appearance and divine pride of the entire supporting and supported mandalas. For people like us in the beginning, for a short while, we should set aside visualizing the other faces and arms and try to visualize clearly only the principal face, two hands, two feet, and the color of [Heruka's] body and try to hold the mind unwaveringly on the [simplified aspect] with one face and two hands without the ornaments. Concerning this method, when we are able to have a generic image of merely the coarse aspects of the face, hands, and body color appear a few times, we should be content with that and, without trying to overanalyze, engage in single-pointed placement meditation.

[Heruka's body] is like the color of the [dark blue] sky. His three eyes are red and move swiftly. His face has a smiling demeanor, and his bared fangs are slightly revealed. He does not appear like a painting or like something made of clay or stone, nor is he something that can be touched as if he were made out of mud. He is slender where [he should be] slender, and thick where [he should be] thick. His body should be proportionate, with a nice shape, without any imperfections or wrinkles, just like a nursing baby.[71] Without inner organs, he is the nature of light, empty on the inside.

Hold that visualization with the mind without following after any others; mentally sustain the root visualization. As for the visualization, if one part is clear, hold it. If it should start to become unclear or the appearance disappears altogether, hold a visualization of the body in general.

Meditate in this way on the appearance [of the deity] and, with the thought "I am the deity," generate strong divine pride. In this state alternate between single-pointed placement meditation on divine pride [and clear appearance]. If you succeed in that, train sequentially in visualizing the [deity] all at once, complete with all the faces and hands, as well as all the hand implements, ornaments, and so forth. If you succeed in that, try visualizing one of the other deities, then add two more, and so on. Then train in visualizing them all at once. Next, train in clarity of the two [sets] of armor, the celestial mansion, and so forth.

By training your mind in this way, if an imbalance in the bodily elements or other such conditions does not arise, and you are able to overcome mental sinking and excitement by thinking of yourself as the deity, with mental stabilization on clear appearance and divine pride, without interruption for one sixth of a day, it is said that you will have attained stability in clear appearance and divine pride. The methods for dispelling mental sinking and excitement should be extracted from the lamrim [teachings].

Sustaining continuously the visualization of the supporting and supported mandalas with a consciousness ascertaining the absence of inherent existence is said to be the method for training in the yoga of nondual profundity and clarity of the generation stage.

---

71. Just as a fresh, newborn baby who is still nursing has such supple and soft skin, so should Heruka be visualized.

How to End the Session

This has four parts:

1. How to Engage in the Recitation
2. How to Offer the Tormas
3. How to Withdraw [the Visualization]
4. How to Make the Dedication Prayers

How to Engage in the Recitation

This has four parts:

1. Blessing the Rosary for Recitation
2. Visualization [during] the Recitation
3. How to Engage in the Recitation
4. Ending the Recitation

Blessing the Rosary for Recitation

Recite, "The faults of meditation . . ." and so forth.[72] In order to keep the number of recitations, obtain a rosary made from human bone or bodhi seeds—suitable for all actions—strung together by a string made by an undefiled[73] young girl. The generation ritual is as follows.

In an instant the rosary transforms into Pāmanarteshvara, who has a red-colored body, one face, and four hands; the right two hands hold a lotus and damaru, and the left two hold a bell and a skull cup together with a katvanga. He has three eyes, is naked, with loose hair, adorned with the five mudras, and stands with his right leg outstretched. He melts into light and transforms into the aspect of a rosary. Imagine inside each bead, from a letter HUM comes a Heruka. As you pull [the beads of] the rosary toward you with your thumb and forefinger, you should imagine

---

72. This line is not found in our sadhana.
73. This refers to a virgin.

the thumb is like a hook and that a duplicate of Heruka is drawn out and dissolves into you.

Visualization [during] the Recitation

Recite, "The commitment recitation . . ." and so forth.[74] It is said that one should do the commitment recitation for the Father and Mother and the heap recitation for the retinue. That is the method [explained] here. At the heart of each deity is a sun seat upon which is a blue letter HUM. This is surrounded by both the Father's and Mother's close-essence mantras on the inside, with the essence mantras outside of that. Visualize at the heart of each of the four goddesses the essence mantras that correspond to the color of their bodies, beginning in front and circling counterclockwise. Next, while reciting the mantra of the Father and Mother, the HUM in the center has five parts: from the drop together with a nada come the Father and Mother; from the crescent moon, Dakini; from the head of the HA, Rupini; from the body of the HA, Kandharohi; from the shabkyu U letter, Lama. Thus limitless numbers of mandala deities radiate out. Or [alternatively you can imagine] that, from the HUM together with the mantra rosary, light rays radiate, and on the tips of those light rays are Heruka Father and Mother in union, complete with all the faces and hands,[75] or with one face and two hands. [Either way] limitless numbers radiate out from the right nostril of your main face. Light rays from your body go to all worldly environments. White and red bodhichitta descend from the joined organs and purify the negative karma, obscurations, and faults of all living beings. All environments transform into the celestial mansion, and all beings become Heruka Father and Mother. The bodies of all the deities as well as the light rays collect back, enter through your left nostril, and dissolve into the letter HUM abiding at your heart. Once again, five-colored light rays radiate as before, and on the tips of these light rays are offering goddesses holding offering substances. They emanate to the ten directions and present offerings to all the buddhas and bodhisattvas.

74. This also does not appear in our sadhana.
75. This means four faces and twelve arms.

All the blessings of their bodies collect back in the aspect of Heruka and dissolve into the crown of your head. All the blessings of their speech collect back in the aspect of mantras and seed syllables and dissolve into your throat. All the blessings of their minds collect back in the aspect of hand implements and dissolve into your heart. In this way imagine that the blessings of the three secrets of the conquerors and their children enter you. This represents the commitment recitation.

As for the visualization for the recitation of the retinue's mantra with the heap of light, if you mentally hold the blazing letters while reciting [the mantra], it will [bestow] quick attainments. This method of recitation is from the teachings of Lalita.[76] Recite the mantras without distraction. When reciting [the mantra, recite it] neither too slowly nor too quickly, neither too distinctly nor too indistinctly [neither too loudly nor too softly]; don't recite the long syllables as short or the short as long; don't interrupt the [recitation] by conversing with others, and don't let the mind wander and so forth. You should be free of any of these faults [of recitation]. It is taught that, while reciting all these mantras, you should imagine that they are being recited together in unison by all four faces of the Principal as well as the mouths of the retinue.

As for the number of recitations, for merely an "action-permitting retreat," you should recite the essence mantra of the Father and Mother one hundred thousand times each, recite any number of the close-essence mantra, and recite the retinue and wisdom-descending mantras ten thousand times each, then perform a compensating, pacifying fire puja to the best of your ability. If you are visualizing the abbreviated wisdom-descending mantra [recite as follows]: OM HRIH HA HA HUM HUM PHAT OM TIKTRA MAHA KRODRA AHBESHEYA HUM. This is explained as permissible and valid.

As for the visualization [during the wisdom-descending mantra], imagine that, from the letter HUM at your heart, red hooking light rays radiate and invoke all the buddhas, bodhisattvas, heroes, and yoginis in the aspect of the mandala deities of Chakrasamvara, who dissolve into your body like a heavy rain entering through all of your pores, and you become nondual.

---

76. Lalitavajra is a famous mahasiddha of the Yamantaka lineage.

How to Engage in the Recitation

Recite, OM SHRI VAJRA . . . and so forth. OM is the forerunner of the mantra. SHRI means "glorious." VAJRA means "indestructible." HE HE RU KAM means "the play of the blood in the skull cup." HUM HUM PHAT means "summoning his mental continuum." DAKINI DZA LA SHAMBHARAM SOHA means "Please, bind [within me] the collection of dakinis that are the nature of simultaneously born bliss. Establish that in me!" Although the seven letters of the close-essence mantra have no meaning, the HRIH[77] and so forth symbolize the five exalted wisdoms.

The meaning of the essence mantra of the Mother is "Mother Vajra Vairochana." And the meaning of the close-essence mantra is "the perfectly praised Vajradakini of all the buddhas."

The mantra of the four goddesses is explained as follows: DAKINIYE means "sky-goer." LAME means "beautiful goddess." KHADHAROHI means "portion-born goddess." RUPINIYE means "form goddess." It is taught that one must remember the meaning of the mantras while reciting them.

Ending the Recitation

Recite the hundred-syllable mantra of Heruka. At the hearts of each lord of the lineage is a moon seat upon which is a HUM surrounded by the hundred-syllable mantra going counterclockwise. From that a stream of nectar descends and enters through the crown of your head, and the excess overflows. All faults such as the excesses and omissions are expelled in the aspect of smoke, ash, and so forth. In this way imagine that you are completely purified and the blessings are stabilized.

How to Offer the Tormas

It is said one should make effort to make torma offerings to the mundane and supramundane guests meaningfully when you are tired. The lord of

---

77. The close-essence mantra is OM HRIH HA HA HUM HUM PHAT. If you remove the OM at the beginning and the PHAT at the end, there are five remaining syllables; these represent the five exalted wisdoms.

the teachings Gelong Jamyang in his *Clear Bliss* explains how to make both brief and extensive [torma offerings].

Furthermore, in the *Samvarodaya Tantra* it says,

> From a torma without intoxicants,
> There will not be swift attainments.
> Therefore it is said that a torma [with intoxicants]
> Is perfectly praised by all the previous buddhas.

In Panchen Chökyi Gyaltsen's text it also says, "Between the sessions one should offer the tormas to the mundane and supramundane [guests]." Since it is Je Lama's intention that you shouldn't do the dissolution before making the [torma] offering, [I will explain] that method here.

Since the torma is said to be the root of all attainments, it should be offered continuously, but especially during a retreat; therefore, it would be best to make a complete [torma offering] during all the sessions. That would really be wonderful. If that is not possible, at least offer one torma at the end of the session. If you don't offer one, you will incur a fault of contradicting your training in secret mantra.

Bless the torma and offerings for the mundane and supramundane [guests]. Recite, "PHAIM. From the letter HUM at my heart, light rays radiate and invoke the directional protectors, field protectors, nagas, and so forth, who abide in the eight charnel grounds together with the mandala of Heruka five deity to the space before me."

Concerning the visualization, while appearing clearly as Heruka, imagine that in the space before you are the guests of the torma offering—the supporting and supported mandalas of Heruka five deity and so forth—with blessed tongues. Simultaneously imagine that from the letter HUM at your heart a limitless number of red vajra goddesses holding skull cups emanate. With the skull cups they scoop up the blessed tormas. Imagine that from the tongues [of the guests] come tubes of light. As a preliminary, make the lotus-turning mudra and then a skull-cup-vessel mudra.

Recite OM VAJRA AH RA LI HO: DZA HUM BAM HO. Saying this means, "The nature of four bodies is the display of the vajra."

Recite VAJRA DAKINI SAMAYATON TRISHAYA HO. Saying this means, "The dakinis generate delight with the *samaya* thought." The first time you say this [mantra] you offer the torma to the Father, the second time to the Mother, and the third time to the retinue.

Next, make the offerings from AHRHGAM up to SHAPTA. Recite the close-essence mantras of the Father, Mother, and the four dakinis, and add the three seed syllables and offer the inner offering. Recite praises with the "eight lines of praise" in Tibetan [or English]. As for the meaning of the verse "You who have destroyed equally existence . . .," it is as follows. The worldly existence and the peace of nirvana are both equal within emptiness. Through [Heruka's] compassion he does not abide in the peace of nirvana, and through his wisdom he does not abide in samsara. Hence, this signifies that by his great compassion, he has destroyed attachment to the extreme of nirvana, and through his great wisdom, he has destroyed all conceptions of existence. He does not grasp at the entity of the object or all phenomena but views them with his spacelike vision as not inherently existing.

"Protector, your mind is heavy with your extreme love, and by the waters of your great compassion may my mental continuum be saturated by that moisture. Likewise may I also be cared for by the love of the goddesses, and through that may they become my friends on the path." Say this clearly and visualize that all your wishes have been fulfilled.

Next, the gods, nagas, givers of harm, cannibals, demigods, sky-dwelling humans, or the toche chenpo[78] who abide in the eight charnel grounds in the cardinal and intermediate directions melt gradually from above and below, dissolve into light, instantly enter the clear light, and arise in the bodily aspect of Heruka Father and Mother with one face and two hands. The vajra-rasa goddesses offer the torma as before.

As for the meaning of the torma mantra, OM is the "three vajras." KA KA means "eat, eat." KHA HI KHA HI is the imperative "eat, eat!" SARWA YASKHA means "all harm givers." Saying "all" clarifies that the same reasoning should be applied to the remaining seven. RAKYASA means "cannibal." BHUTA is "harmful spirit." PRETA is "hungry ghost." PISHATSA means "flesh eater." UNATA is "crazy maker." APAMARA is "forgetful maker." VAJRA DAKA means "male sky traveler." DAKINADYA means "female sky traveler." IMAM BALING GRIHANTU means "seize

---

78. Tib. *lto phye chen po*.

this torma." SAMAYA RAKYANTU means "protecting the commitments." MAMA SARWA SIDDHI METRA YATZANTU means "please bestow upon me all of the best attainments." YATIPAM means "in this way." YATETAM means "moreover." BHUDZATA means "requesting one's desires." PIWATA means "drink." DZAGATRA[79] means "brandish." MATITRAMATA means "through the stages of thought." MAMA SARWA KATAYA means "all of my actions." SADSUKHAM BISHUDAYE means "the sacred pure bliss." SAHAYEKA BHAWENTU means "may the guests please bestow the attainments." Recite this twice and offer the torma to the eight groups of the Principal and his retinue. Offer to those in the directions counterclockwise and to those in the intermediate directions clockwise.

Make the outer offerings with AHRGHAM and so forth. Offer the inner offering with "To the mouths of the directional guardian, regional guardians, nagas, and so forth, OM AH HUM."

Next, recite, "For the sake of protecting the teachings . . ." and so forth. Imagine that you are making the request for the four enlightened actions.

Recite OM VARJA MU and at the same time with the back of your left hand [facing you] snap the thumb and forefinger together three times and imagine that the worldly guests return to their own places.

Then recite, "OM YOGA SHUDDHA . . ." and so forth, and imagine that the supramundane guests of the torma and the supporting and supporting [mandalas] dissolve into you. If making an abbreviated torma offering, apply the same reasoning.[80]

How to Withdraw [the Visualization]

Recite the dissolution section [from the sadhana]. This will be explained in accordance with *Illuminating Bliss*. Recite, "From the HUM at my heart . . ." and so forth. From the letter HUM at your heart, countless red light rays radiate, cleansing the faults of the environment and its beings. The worldly environment melts into light and dissolves into the celestial mansion. The sentient beings who are its inhabitants dissolve

---

79. This spelling varies from that in the sadhana.
80. This is clearly laid out in the sadhana.

into the supported deity. The celestial mansion together with the charnel grounds and protection circle melt into light and dissolve into the retinue. The retinue also melts into light and dissolves into the southeastern skull cup, which dissolves into Dakini in the east. She melts into light and dissolves into the root face of the Principal. Likewise, the northeastern [skull cup] and the northern [goddess] dissolve into the left face. In the same way, the northwestern [skull cup] and the western [goddess] dissolve into the rear face. The southwestern [skull cup] and the southern [goddess] dissolve into the right face. These melt into light and dissolve into the four faces [of Heruka] sequentially. Again, the bodies of the Father and Mother melt into light in stages from above and below and dissolve into the letter HUM at their heart. The letter HUM completely transforms, and you arise in the body of Heruka with one face and two hands. The moon at your crown is marked by a white letter OM. The lotus at your throat is marked by a red letter AH. The sun at your heart is marked by a blue letter HUM. Imagine that you become marked with these [seed syllables].

Therefore, concerning the need for doing this, through the force of meditation during the completion stage, all of the winds will dissolve into the indestructible drop at your heart, whereby the example and meaning clear lights will dawn. From that you will attain the pure and impure illusory bodies, and it is said that this must become a ripening agent for your roots of virtue [for accomplishing the completion stage].

How to Make the Dedication Prayers

Recite, "Glorious Heruka, your body…" and so forth. The meaning of these three verses is as follows. Due to the desire elicited by embracing the Mother Vajravarahi, light rays from your body emanate as the fire of exalted wisdom that blazes below the ground, above the ground, and on the ground. The blazing light rays of your body [pervade] the three realms. Heruka's long and narrow eyes [indicate] his disciplined mood. From his dark blue body, many thousands of blue light rays radiate, blazing as magnificently as one hundred thousand suns shining all at once. From his body and attire arise emanations, which do not arise in only one way. Instead, they manifest to subdue [sentient beings] in whatever way the many sentient beings [need them], and care for them through the power of his great love and compassion and reveal these all at once. His mental continuum is the exalted wisdom of nondual bliss and emptiness. As an external sign of his power, he suppresses Bhairava and Kalarati under his feet and has a heroic mood. In the same way the exalted wisdom of nondual bliss and emptiness of Heruka's mind will dance simultaneously with you in the future. Through their nondeceptive realization of emptiness, the goddesses are valid. Since they have not transgressed the words of Vajradhara, they have valid commitments. They are supremely valid teachings if they have been accomplished in accordance with the words of truth proclaimed by a sage. The goddesses endowed with these truths will care for you throughout all your lives. The former recitations, praises, and so forth, thereby become the roots of virtue.

Recite the next dedication verse:

> To accomplish the welfare of all living beings,
> May I become Heruka,
> And then lead every living being
> To Heruka's supreme state.

Hence, make the dedication prayers each day, and when reciting self-generation alone recite the auspicious prayer "Bliss and excellence..." and so forth.[81]

How to Practice During the Meditation Break

From within the state of not being separated from the state of divine pride as Heruka, all worlds and all living beings that you see, hear, and so forth, should be viewed as the supporting and supported mandalas of Heruka Chakrasamvara while abiding in the Brahmin conduct.[82] When seeing the bodies of the guru, buddhas, bodhisattvas, and so forth, you should imagine them as Chakrasamvara, recite the "eight lines of praise,"

---

81. This auspicious prayer does not appear in our sadhana.

82. Brahmin conduct has two primary implications: one is that of celibacy and the other of engaging in all actions with pure appearance and divine pride. It is the latter that is being emphasized here.

and make prostrations. For the sake of increasing the concentration of bliss and emptiness, view all wheels[83] in the three realms as bound by the inseparable nature of simultaneously born supreme bliss and emptiness. Desiring good qualities in general and special entities [in particular], meditate on the form of the consort and so forth, and enjoy the objects of desire like a fearless lion. Through this you increase the body which stabilizes and increases bliss, and from that great bliss the uncommon concentration [of bliss and emptiness] increases. Thus, by abiding in the concentration of the state of glorious Heruka, all movements of the body, all proclamations of speech, and all thoughts are bound by mudra and are like mantra recitation, and in that way you complete your collection [of merit and wisdom].

In *All Conducts* it says,

> Abiding in the state of Shri Heruka
> You will discover that all
> Limitless movements of the limbs and speech
> Are mudra and secret mantra.

Such are the principal concentrations during the meditation breaks, and if you become well acquainted, when you are directly enjoying the five objects of the senses, they will manifest as the concentration of bliss and emptiness. If your mental engagements are impeded by ordinary appearances, it will be incompatible with great bliss. Therefore, binding the doors of the senses is said to be the supreme moral discipline of the path in this tradition. Moreover, one easily completes the collection of merit and ripens the roots of virtue for generating supreme realizations of the completion stage and so forth; thus it is said there are limitless benefits.

When sleeping, as done [during the sadhana], collect [everything] into the letter HUM. This dissolves sequentially from below into the nada. The nada [dissolves] into unobservable, inseparable bliss and emptiness, and imagine that this becomes the truth body; then go to sleep. Upon rising

---

83. "Wheels" is a translation of the Sanskrit word *chakra*, which constitutes the first part of the name Chakrasamvara. It refers to all objects of knowledge.

during the third part of the dawn on the next day, imagine that the dakinis, Vajravarahi, and so forth, are playing damarus and singing songs and you are awakened from the clear light and arise in the form body [of Heruka]. From your heart, light rays radiate and invoke washing goddesses holding vases who bestow empowerment. All the sickness, harm from spirits, negative karma, and obscurations are cleansed, and you generate bliss and emptiness as you wash your hands and mouth. Having blessed your food and drink in accordance with the inner offering, imagine that all the deities are collected into the essence of the letter HUM at your heart, and by making offerings, they are satiated by great bliss. In this way enjoy [your food and drink].

As stated in the *Four Seats Tantra*:

> Whatever small amount of food and drink
> That you eat after having dedicated it;
> For the yogi who enjoys in this way,
> It does not become a [karmic] debt.[84]

This was already explained earlier during the stage of offering a torma to the mundane and supramundane [guests].

Thus your entire behavior must not be allowed to be ordinary, but you should train in pure appearances and conceptions.

For this purpose Kaychok Pawo says,

> Through the continuous, unbroken yoga,
> One should make effort to accomplish concentration.

One must make effort like a continuous river in divine pride and clear appearance of the generation stage and not let it be interrupted by other distractions, whether virtuous, nonvirtuous, or neutral. It is said that if you meditate continuously, it will not take longer than one year to complete [your training in generation stage]. And it will not take long to perfect it.

---

84. "Debt" here refers to being karmically indebted to those who provide you with food. If you offer food to yourself as Heruka, you don't incur such a karmic debt.

THE BENEFITS OF SUCH A MEDITATION

In the *Lamp Illuminating the Five Stages* it says,

> Keep your vows and commitments purely and respect your lama. If you meditate on the supreme deity of the generation stage with fierce devotion for your personal deity, upon your death your own supreme deity will care for you, and you will see the benefits of the Dharma.

Additionally, the obstacles of obstructing spirits will not be able to harm you, and you will quickly complete your collections [of merit and wisdom], you will purify ordinary appearance and conceptions, and the deity will bless your mental continuum and so forth.

Concerning the unique way the mahasiddhas taught the tantra of Heruka, by meditating in four sessions on the generation stage according to the previous explanation and bringing the three bodies into death, intermediate state, and rebirth, you will ripen your mental continuum to generate the complete realization of the completion stage. By penetrating the vital points of the channels, winds, and drops during the generation stage, you will quickly complete the special characteristics of the completion stage so that you may, in this short lifetime, in these degenerate times, attain the state of glorious Heruka—the ground of a tathagata. Even if you don't attain that in this life, you will attain it in a future life. Furthermore, you will be born into a family of the supreme vehicle, and by practicing this Dharma, you will become a devout king. Your previous accumulations of negative karma and obscurations will be purified, and by merely concentrating on this path, reading the [Heruka] scriptures, reciting the recitation, or copying a volume of this tantra, you will attain all the glories of higher rebirth in general, and in particular, it is said that you will become a universal monarch and obtain a kingdom.

If you are lazy and distracted with amusements, although you may not gain realizations, at the time of your death, the yogis and yoginis who are practitioners of this path will be transferred to the pure lands from this world by the dakinis, which will be like moving to a nice home. From belonging to the lineage of this Dharma practice to again belonging to the lineage that practices this Dharma [in your next life], everything else in between will be like merely taking a rest, and "death" will be nothing more than something conventionally labeled by the mind. Don't ever let any regret, fear, or trepidation arise at all when you die. At that time, glorious Guru Heruka, Vajravarahi, and so forth, and the heroes and yoginis, will be holding flowers and incense, victory banners, and a variety of parasols, and with the sound of cymbals and so forth, together with a variety of music and singing pleasing vajra songs, will escort and place the practitioner upon a lion throne. With a tent of rainbow light canopies and a variety of flowers descending like rain, you will be led to the outer abode of Pure Dakini Land. The inner Dakini Land is the transformation of the nature of the clear light of death into the path, in dependence upon which you will manifest the state of union of Heruka.

As the great foremost being [Lama Tsongkhapa] said,

> It is taught that the heroes and yoginis upon this earth who are
> able to actualize these benefits are extremely rare. Therefore,
> at this time when you have found such a practice as this path
> that is very difficult to find, and by understanding how difficult
> it is to find, you should listen, contemplate, and meditate, and
> extract the essence of this life of leisure.

Colophon

Bestowing the three supreme bodies in one short life,
Without having to wait three countless eons of this degenerate age,
Of the one hundred and sixty million yogini tantras,
The final essence is the tantra of Chakrasamvara.

Losang Drakpa and Dharmabhadra
Illuminated this tradition of Mahasiddha Ghantapa
For training in the path of the first stage
In dependence upon the noble text of Chökyi Gyaltsen.

My protector, who is the only eye of migrators in this degenerate age,
Jetsun Chenpo Dharmabhadra Shab,
Taught this method of training in the path of the first stage.

Drinking the words of his teaching from the crown of my head,
If even a mere portion of this explanation that I have put in this diary
Has any mistakes, with regret I confess them before his sacred eyes.

Whatever has been properly assembled is because of the Venerable
Guru, my refuge and protector.
May he have a long life that increases like vajra Mount Meru, and
May the Muni's teachings spread throughout the ten directions.

Here this profound commentary was kindly given by the all-pervasive
lord of the mandala and the lineage, Vajradhara Jetsun Dharmabhadra
Palsangpo in the third month of the Wood Sheep Year (1835).

The Protector's servant, the lowly Gelong Döndrup Gyaltsen, compiled
the notes.

SARVA MANGALAM
May Everything Be Auspicious!

Second Colophon

Once again on a variety of excellent dates of the year, the definitive meaning of the chief of living beings, Lay Lung Lama Rinpoche Gelong Tsultrim Gyaltsen Chok,[85] and the treasurer Tenzin Tsultrim both combined
their money and printed this. During the printing they checked the words
and meaning and made corrections and additions; therefore, whatever
changes have been made should be followed.

---

85. This is the founder of Ganden Kachoe monastery. See www.dechenling.org for more information on the current incarnation of this monastery.

When the previous notes were put together along with the colophon, I was young and it was a difficult task for me since I lacked proper knowledge. As a result, there were many mistakes. Earlier [Yangchen Drupay Dorje] only had the chance to show these corrections to Je Lama once; therefore, his corrections are not confirmed. In the beginning, middle, and end there were a lot of mistakes. So it is that Yangchen Drupay Dorje took over the responsibility so that I could fulfill my promise of completing the text. In the hope that those who wish to practice this path will get some benefit, whatever part of the supreme speech of the Jetsun Lama I was able to remember I wrote down. Also, I examined well many other texts and made additions and changes.

OM SVATI

Of the one hundred and sixteen million yogini tantras,
This is like the foremost tip of a victory banner and
[Contains] all of the profound meanings of
The root and explanatory tantras of Chakrasamvara as it is
Collected into one in the tradition of the supreme siddha
Ghantapa Shab.

The excellent path of the first stage was taught
According to the intention of the methods of training
Of the two conquerors and [taught] by the
All-knowing Dharmabhadra who abundantly bestowed this wondrous,
excellent explanation.

Through the clear intention of the two excellent beings,
And with this ship of instructions for fortunate beings,
One can easily traverse to the jeweled island of the three bodies.

This inexhaustible Dharma is a gift accomplishing the great miracle
From which one attains the white light rays of the sun
That dispels all the darkness of the mind.

May the vessel of my heart be completely filled with

This lotus garland of explanations of experience and realization.

In particular, the pair of benefactors who supplied the resources for
The very essence of this good path of sutra and tantra,
When the appearances of this life finally end,
May they travel to the Pure Dakini Land.

This [poem] was written by Yangchen Drupay Dorje.

May virtue increase.

Translator's Colophon

This text was completed in October 2007. I checked the difficult passages
of the Tibetan text with my former language teacher Lobsang Thonden.
In October 2009, in preparation for publication, I once again checked the
translation for errors and revised the entire translation and made numerous changes. I hope that this text will benefit English-speaking Heruka
practitioners.

Two-armed Chakrasamvara.
Painting by Andy Weber.

EASTERN ENTRANCE TO THE MANDALA OF HERUKA.
Photo courtesy of Joel Fraser.

INTERIOR OF THE MANDALA OF HERUKA.
Photo courtesy of Joel Fraser.

Western entrance to the mandala of Heruka.
Photo courtesy of Joel Fraser.

The Panchen Lama's Commentary to

The Five Stages of Completion

The First Panchen Lama Losang Chökyi Gyaltsen

Introduction to the Panchen Lama's Commentary

U NTIL NOW most of the material concerning the completion stage of highest yoga tantra has been in regard to the six yogas of Naropa[86] and the five stages of Guhyasamaja.[87] Here, for the first time in English, is a translation of the First Panchen Lama's commentary on the five stages of Ghantapa. These are not the same five stages as in Guhyasamaja, yet nevertheless all the five stages of Guhyasamaja are included within the five stages of Ghantapa. The five stages of Guhyasamaja are isolated speech, isolated mind, illusory body, clear light, and union. The five stages of Ghantapa are blessing the self, variegated vajra, filling the jewel, dzalandhara, and yoga of inconceivability.

The first stage, blessing the self, draws the winds into the central channel and allows one to gain control over the winds through vajra recitation. The second stage, variegated vajra, allows one to gain control over the drops. In the third stage, filling the jewel, one learns to work with the four types of mudras: action mudra, wisdom mudra, phenomena mudra, and mahamudra. In the fourth stage, dzalandhara, one gains control over the inner heat. And in the fifth stage, the yoga of inconceivability, one gains control over the mind and progresses through isolated mind, illusory body, clear light, and union.

In this text the first two stages of Guhyasamaja—isolated speech and isolated mind—are included within the first four stages. The last three—illusory body, clear light, and union—are included within the fifth: the yoga of inconceivability.

---

86. For a brilliant presentation of the six yogas of Naropa, see Glenn Mullin's translation of *Tsong-khapa's Six Yogas of Naropa* (Ithaca, NY: Snow Lion Publications, 1996); and *Readings on the Six Yogas of Naropa* (Ithaca, NY: Snow Lion Publications, 1997).

87. For the five stages of Guhyasamaja, see Daniel Cozort, *Highest Yoga Tantra* (Ithaca, NY: Snow Lion Publications, 1986).

The Panchen Lama contributes little to the section concerning the yoga of inconceivability; therefore, I thought it might be helpful to explain a little more about this profound stage of meditation.

It should be noted that, at this point of progression in completion stage meditation, all tantric systems—with the exception of Kalachakra—converge. Whether you are practicing Heruka, Yamantaka, or Guhyasamaja, from this point onward they all follow the same procedure: the two concentrations and the three conducts.

During the previous four stages of meditation, the practitioner was able to draw the winds into the central channel, generate the four joys, and manifest the eight signs from miragelike up to the clear light. Depending on the practitioner, he or she has attained either isolated speech or isolated mind.[88] The first, isolated speech, is attained when the winds are drawn into the central channel at the heart but not into the indestructible drop. The second, isolated mind, has two primary classifications: isolated mind of example clear light and isolated mind of ultimate example clear light.

The first, isolated mind of example clear light, occurs when the winds have been drawn into the indestructible drop at the heart but some of the pervasive wind that permeates the entire body has not. The second, isolated mind of ultimate example clear light, occurs when all the winds have dissolved into the indestructible drop at the heart, yet the mind of clear light is meditating on emptiness through a generic image and not directly.

Meaning clear light occurs when the subtle mind of clear light realizes emptiness directly, and this is counted as stage four of the Guhyasamaja system.

From ultimate example clear light, the impure illusory body manifests, and from meaning clear light, the pure illusory body arises. The impure illusory body is stage three of the Guhyasamaja system, and the pure illusory body is part of stage four—clear light. This is the meaning clear light. Union occurs when, after arising from meaning clear light in the form of

---

88. Earlier it was said that at this point one would have attained isolated mind. However, there are some practitioners who find it very difficult to attain isolated mind in dependence upon the previous stages. Therefore, at this point if they were to engage in the two concentrations and three conducts, they would succeed in attaining isolated mind. There are also those who find it easier to attain isolated mind and may have succeeded in drawing the winds into the indestructible drop at the heart sooner. Either way, at the stage of inconceivability, one will succeed in attaining isolated mind, the impure illusory body, meaning clear light, and union.

the pure illusory body, the practitioner once again enters into meditation and "unifies" the pure illusory body and meaning clear light. In one session one attains meaning clear light and arises in the pure illusory body, and in the very next meditation session, the practitioner attains union. Therefore, the three stages—clear light, illusory body, and union—are attained in two meditation sessions.

There are two stages of union: the union that needs learning and the union of no-more learning. The first is the state of an arya bodhisattva, and the second is the state of full enlightenment. These stages of clear light are attained using the two primary methods mentioned above: the two concentrations and the three conducts.

The two concentrations are "holding the body entirely" and "subsequent destruction." The first occurs when one imagines the body dissolving into the indestructible drop at the heart and then mediates on the clear light. The second occurs when the whole universe dissolves into one's body, and then the body dissolves as before.

The three conducts constitute various ways of relying on either an action mudra—a physical consort, or a wisdom mudra—a visualized consort. These various ways include with elaboration, without elaboration, and completely without elaboration. The first uses various consorts, dances, costumes, and so forth. The second relies on only one consort, while the third relies on a merely visualized consort, or wisdom mudra.

Through the two concentrations and three conducts, one is able to progress through the varying degrees of realization of emptiness with the mind of clear light, the two illusory bodies, the union of the clear light and illusory body, and finally full enlightenment. All of these meditations are included in the fifth stage, the stage of inconceivability.

As we can see, the five stages of Ghantapa contain all of the profound instructions of the six yogas of Naropa as well as the five stages of Guhyasamaja, while expounding on the yoga of the drops and relying on the four types of mudras. Therefore, the five stages of Ghantapa provide a rich and valuable structure for meditating on the completion stage.

This text by the First Panchen Lama Losang Chökyi Gyaltsen is one of the most highly guarded "sealed in secrecy" texts within the Gelugpa tradition.[89] It is not included in the Panchen Lama's collected works. Instead, the woodblocks are preserved by the abbot of Tashi Lhunpo Monastery who is only allowed to let two people make copies each year.

As it mentions in the colophon,

> Also, each year there cannot be more than two copies made.
> If you exceed more than that, the guardians and dharma protectors possessing power and ability will annihilate you with their wrath.

Later, more copies were printed by Pabongkha Rinpoche and Trijang Rinpoche, but still it was very difficult to obtain a copy of the text. My guru—Gen Lobsang Choephel—was given a copy of this text by Trijang Rinpoche, and Gen-la in turn gave me his copy as well as the transmission of the text and practice. I then translated the text as a way of studying the material in more depth. A few years later when completing the commentary to the Heruka five deity practice by Ngulchu Dharmabhadra, which deals only with the generation stage, it occurred to me that to include this text by the Panchen Lama would complete the text wonderfully. I then approached Gen Lobsang Choephel to seek his permission to publish the text. He responded: "This commitment not to publish more than two copies a year is not something that can effectively be maintained in this day and age. If we did, the text would disappear. This way people, or more specifically, Heruka practitioners, will have access to this important text that they may otherwise not even hear about."

One of the unique features of this commentary is its beautiful and detailed guru yoga method as a way of preparing the mind for meditation on the completion stage. As with all tantric practice, the emphasis is on the guru viewed in the pure aspect of Buddha Vajradhara.

Technically speaking, this text is part of the body mandala system of Mahasiddha Ghantapa. The five stages of completion stage of Ghantapa are exactly the same for the five deities as they are for the body mandala. The difference lies in the point at which one undertakes the practice.

---

89. For a brief biography of Panchen Losang Chökyi Gyaltsen (1567–1662), see Janis. D. Willis, *Enlightened Beings* (Boston: Wisdom Publications, 1995).

In tantric practice there are clearly defined stages of meditation: the generation stage and the completion stage. The generation stage consists of two parts: gross and subtle. The first entails the visualization of the entire supporting and supported mandalas held in meditative equipoise. The second—the subtle generation stage—entails visualizing the entire mandala in a tiny drop at either the upper or lower end of the central channel. This quickly brings a state of single-pointed meditation that swiftly results in the attainment of tranquil abiding. Furthermore, since the winds are drawn into the central channel, one naturally progresses from the subtle generation stage to the completion stage. At this point one would undertake the meditation described in this text.

Since the body mandala has a unique method for blessing the channels, winds, and drops, it is permissible to engage in scanning meditation on the completion stage at the end of your session on the generation stage. Within the five deity practice, there is no such method for blessing the channels, winds, and drops; therefore, before actually undertaking this practice, one must have completed the gross and subtle generation stage.

Also, regardless of the way in which one arrives at this point, one must receive the transmission, the oral instructions, and permission to engage in the completion stage; it is not something that you just wake up one day and decide to do. You must proceed carefully under the guidance of your lama.

Nevertheless, reading this text, understanding it, and gaining an appreciation for its method places deep and powerful imprints in the mind, which will ultimately result in your enlightenment. We should approach this text with the sense of wonder and awe with which it has been maintained for the last several hundred years. We are extremely fortunate to be able to read such a valued and rare text as this.

The Extremely Profound Commentary to the Five Stages of the Profound Tradition of the Powerful Siddha Ghantapa

With great respect I prostrate to the lotus feet of the guru, inseparable
    from the supreme deity,
And request the heroes and dakinis to please patiently care for me
    throughout all my lives.

To the supreme guru and Chakrasamvara,
Respectfully I prostrate at your lotus feet.

May the ten million heroes and dakinis lead me through this narrow
    passage
As I write this commentary to the profound five stages.

Here, I shall compose a precise commentary on the profound and essential points concerning the stages of visualization for the five stages of the completion stage of Chakrasamvara in the tradition of Mahasiddha Ghantapa Shab.

This has two parts:

    1. THE PRELIMINARIES
    2. THE ACTUAL PRACTICE

<hr>

The Actual Practice

1. The Common [Preliminaries]
2. The Uncommon [Preliminaries]

The Common Preliminaries

Train your mental continuum in the common path, obtain perfectly the outer and inner four empowerments of glorious Chakrasamvara, and strive to protect properly the vows and commitments taken at the time of the empowerment.

The Uncommon Preliminaries

This has two parts:

1. Cleansing the Negative Karma, Obscurations, and Unfavorable Conditions through Meditation and Recitation of Vajrasattva
2. Establishing Favorable Conditions by Accumulating Merit through Guru Yoga

Cleansing the Negative Karma, Obscurations, and Unfavorable Conditions through Meditation and Recitation of Vajrasattva

Go for refuge by saying:

"To the Buddha, Dharma and Sangha . . ." and so forth.

Generate bodhichitta by saying:

"For the welfare of all sentient beings . . ." and so forth.

From among the four opponent powers, this is the "power of reliance." As a preliminary, recite the four immeasurables.

The Meditation and Recitation of Vajrasattva

In the beginning you must meditate on the generation stage with all the essential features of bringing the three bodies into the path that is concordant with the mental continuum of [death, intermediate stage, and] rebirth, as well as the ripening agent, the purified basis, and the purifier in accordance with the sadhana.

Then from the final dissolution of the clear light, arise in the aspect of Heruka Father and Mother with one face and two hands. Above the crown of your head at the peak of your topknot, the nature of the exalted wisdom of inseparable bliss and emptiness appears in the aspect of a white letter PAM. This melts into light [and transforms into] a white eight-petaled lotus with a red luster; the center is green and the corolla is orange and extremely luminous. Upon this, the nature of the exalted wisdom of inseparable bliss and emptiness in the aspect of a white short vowel AH melts into light and [transforms] into a moon mandala, white, full, and cool, like a mirror standing upright. Upon this, the nature of the nondual exalted wisdom of the minds of all the buddhas in the aspect of a white letter HUM melts into light and arises as a white, five-spoked vajra, in the center of which is a letter HUM radiating limitless rays of light. On the tips of each light ray are offering goddesses with a variety of offering substances in their hands, making offerings to all the buddhas and bodhisattvas in the ten directions and producing extraordinary uncontaminated bliss in their mental continuums. On the tip of each light ray radiate Vajrasattva Father and Mother, in a number equal to the extent of sentient beings, and they then abide at the crown of each sentient being. From the joined organs [of all the Vajrasattvas] a stream of bodhichitta nectar descends, filling the inside of all [sentient beings'] bodies and overflowing outside; thereby they are all washed. All negative karma, obscurations, their seeds, and their imprints are dispelled like a lamp [dispelling] darkness or are expelled outside through the doors of the senses and all the hair pores in the aspect of liquid coal or liquid smoke. Vajrasattva Father and Mother dissolve into the crown of each sentient being, and they are established in the state of Vajrasattva. All the buddhas and bodhisattvas collect back and dissolve into the vajra and the letter HUM, which completely transforms into Vajrasattva Father and Mother.

Generate them thus in accord with the ritual. Then:

Imagine in the center of their crown chakra is a white OM, the nature of the vajra body of all the tathagatas. At the center of their throat chakra is a red AH, the nature of vajra speech. The center of their heart chakra is marked by a blue HUM, the nature of the vajra mind.

At their heart in the center of a moon mandala is a white letter HUM, surrounded by the hundred-syllable mantra, arranged in a rosary standing upright, from which limitless light rays radiate. The wisdom beings in the aspect of form bodies identical to the meditation beings are invoked from their natural abodes of the dharmakaya. DZA HUM BAM HO, they are invoked; they enter, are bound, and are then empowered. Bestow empowerment and seal them [with the lord of the lineage] according to the ritual [from the Heruka sadhana]. As before, develop regret for your negative karma and downfalls as the power of destruction. Then imagine the three spheres [are the nature of emptiness] by remembering that the negative karma is empty of inherent existence; recalling this meaning is the "power of opposing force."

Then with that understanding, request:

"Bhagawan Vajrasattva, please cleanse and purify all our negative karma, obscurations, and broken and degenerated vows and commitments."

Having requested in this way, from the mantra rosary and letter HUM at their hearts, limitless light rays radiate, and on the tip of each light ray emanate limitless Father and Mother Vajrasattvas, equal to the number of sentient beings. They abide at the crown of the head of each sentient being, and from the joined organs of the Father and Mother, nectar descends, cleansing instantly all the darkness, negative karma, obscurations, and imprints. These are dispelled through the lower doors and the hair pores in the aspect of liquid coal and liquid smoke, and they [sentient beings] are then established in the state of Vajrasattva. Once again, limitless light rays radiate, and on the tip of each light ray are offering goddesses with various offering substances in their hands. They offer them to all the buddhas and bodhisattvas, and they generate uncontaminated extraordinary bliss in their mental continua. Again, stringlike light rays radiate, reaching the hearts of all the conquerors, from which come all the good qualities of their body, speech, and mind in the aspect of light rays and nectar, which arise and coil around [the string] and dissolve into the mantra rosary and letter HUM. Then that nectar descends and enters through the Brahma aperture [at your crown], filling your whole body with the nectar of exalted wisdom, and you imagine all your negative karma and obscurations are cleansed and purified. Accomplish any number of recitations of the hundred-syllable mantra.

Afterward with single-pointed mind say:

"Due to my ignorance and unknowing..."

Then say:

"I go for refuge to the chief of sentient beings..." up to "From now on I will not commit them again."

Saying [these words] with a mind of restraint serves as the power of "turning away from nonvirtue."

Then from the mouth of Vajrasattva:

"Child of the lineage, all your negative karma, obscurations, and broken and degenerated vows and commitments are cleansed and purified."

From the seed syllable at his heart, light rays radiate and summon all the buddhas and bodhisattvas in the ten directions and all sentient beings as Vajrasattva, and they all dissolve into the crown of Vajrasattva at your crown. Father and Mother enter into embrace, and the bodhichitta melts and enters through the crown of your head, descends through the path of your central channel, and dissolves into your mind in the aspect of the indestructible drop at your heart. Imagine your very subtle three doors become inseparable from the body, speech, and mind of Vajrasattva.

Meditation on Guru Yoga

As above, you arise in the body of Heruka Father and Mother with one face and two hands. At the tip of your topknot of hair is an extremely vast, precious jeweled throne upheld by eight snow lions. Upon this is a letter PAM that melts into light and transforms into an eight-petaled lotus of various colors that symbolizes not being polluted by the faults of samsara. In the center of this is the nature of the method of the exalted wisdom of great bliss in the aspect of a red letter RAM that melts and arises as a sun mandala. Upon this, symbolizing the exalted wisdom of emptiness, is a white letter AH, which melts and arises as a moon mandala. Upon this is my root guru, who is of the nature of all the buddhas of the three times, in the aspect of all-pervasive conqueror Vajradhara, with a blue-colored body, one face, and two hands. His right hand holds a vajra, and his left a bell. He embraces the Mother Vajradhatu Ishvari, who has a blue-colored body, holds a curved knife and skull cup, and embraces the Father. They both have precious jeweled crown ornaments, ear ornaments, necklaces, bracelets, and anklets and are adorned with a variety of precious jewels. Their upper bodies are draped in fine silks, and their lower bodies with garments; they are adorned with the thirty-two major marks and eighty minor indications. The Father sits in the vajra position, and the Mother in the lotus position. Seeing their bodies dispels all unknowing. I will never be satisfied looking at their bodies. The mere sight of them causes an afterglow of goose bumps. His speech possesses sixty melodies by which he can answer all questions with one voice so that all understand it in their own language. His mind of inconceivable exalted wisdom knows both conventional and ultimate realities. With his great love he views all living beings with compassion as if each were his only child.

[Then praise him by saying:]

The ornament wheels of your body, speech, and mind are inexhaustible secrets. Your five aggregates are the five [buddha] families. Your four elements are the four mothers. Your sources, joints, and so forth, are male and female bodhisattvas. Your limbs are the wrathful protectors. Your twenty-one thousand pores are in essence Mahayana arhats, and all of your pores are filled with buddhas and bodhisattvas appearing as a limitless array of buddha lands beyond measure, countless, equaling the atoms in the worldly realms. You reveal inconceivable emanations of your body, speech, and mind, enacting the twelve deeds, purifying all realms, and turning the vast wheel of Dharma according to the fortune of each sentient being, fulfilling the immeasurable needs of migrating beings. In short, your body appears in all realms, and the array of your body, speech, and mind, as well as your enlightened actions, pervades all realms, displaying immeasurable miracles.

Visualize that at his crown, in the center of the channel wheel, on a moon, is a white OM. At his throat, in the center of the channel wheel, on a lotus, is a red AH. At his heart, in the center of the channel wheel, on a sun, is a blue HUM. From the HUM at his heart, limitless light rays radiate to the ten directions and invoke the lineage gurus, peaceful and wrathful deities, and a limitless collection of deities, buddhas, and bodhisattvas, surrounded by a collection of heroes, dakinis, and dharma protectors who dissolve into your root guru in the aspect of Vajradhara.

DZA, HUM, BAM, HO

They become nondual with the commitment beings.

The guru is the embodiment of all gurus,
The embodiment of all deities,
The embodiment of all dharma protectors.
In short, his nature is the embodiment of all three [objects]
of refuge.

The seven limbs of complete purity for accumulation and purification begin with prostration. With your mind [recall how] your root guru is endowed with the three types of kindness. He is the embodiment of all the compassion, power, and wisdom of all the buddhas of the three times without exception and has exhausted all faults and is endowed with all good qualities. He is the root of all attainments, the source of all benefit and happiness. Merely hearing his name protects you from the misery of samsara and nirvana. By relying on him with faith and seeing the nature of his actions [as pure], the common and supreme attainments will be bestowed in one lifetime. He has emanations equal to the atoms of his body. And if there were one hundred thousand million bodies and each one had a mouth and each mouth had a hundred thousand million tongues, still they could not count the number of his emanations. Imagine each one of these expressing at one time the good qualities of the body, speech, and mind of your guru.

[Recite the praise:]

"By whose kindness the state of great bliss . . ." and so forth.

His complete enjoyment body is ablaze with the glory of the magnificent signs and indications.

While saying this, make prostrations.

The Branch of Offering

From your heart emanate offering goddesses holding a variety of offering substances. Imagine that they make offerings such as the four waters and a variety of offering substances and so forth. Recite the verse for offering water for drinking and so forth. [Offer] the close enjoyment offerings of music, the five objects of desire, and the inner offering, which is the nature of the five meats and five nectars, that is blessed and subsequently offered. Then, offer a knowledge goddess possessing the characteristics who dissolves into Vajradhatu Ishvari. Through the joy of Father and Mother entering into embrace, they generate uncontaminated bliss in their mental continua. That bliss [realizes] definitive emptiness and becomes inseparable bliss and emptiness; this is the offering of suchness. [In this way], offer the outer and inner offerings in the aspect of the offering substance while their nature is inseparable bliss and emptiness. Through this, uncontaminated exalted bliss is generated in the minds of the subject of the offerings, and through the power of these offerings possessing the three special [qualities], their minds become pleased and satiated.

[SEVEN COMPLETE PURITIES, MANDALA OFFERING, AND RECEIVING THE FOUR EMPOWERMENTS]

Purify your negative karma, downfalls, and their imprints accumulated since beginningless lives by generating fierce regret as before. Then, developing a very strong mind of restraint, make the determination that you will not engage in [such negative karma] again for the rest of your life, and make confession. Meditate by rejoicing in the roots of virtues of yourself and others. Then request the [buddhas] to turn the wheel of the vast and profound Dharma of the Mahayana for the sake of disciples. Request them not to pass into a state of nirvana but to remain for as long as sentient beings exist; then finally dedicate all your virtue for the unsurpassed state of enlightenment.

Say:

"Without control I have engaged in nonvirtue and . . ."

Or:

"Under the power of attachment, hatred, and ignorance . . ."

Say these not merely from the mouth, but with a subdued mind, and recite the seven complete purities.

Next, offer a mandala with four continents, Mount Meru, the seven precious possessions of a king, offering goddesses, and your own body, enjoyments, and virtues of the three times, all without exception, and fill all three thousand [worlds] perfectly with your visualization, instead of something meager.

With stable visualization emanate with your mind a great land, and then make the following request:

I request you, my precious guru, whose nature is the embodiment of all buddhas.
I request you, my precious guru, whose nature is the embodiment of all holy Dharma.
I request you, my precious guru, whose nature is the embodiment of all Sangha.
I request you, my precious guru, whose nature is the embodiment of all deities.
I request you, my precious guru, whose nature is the embodiment of all Three [Jewels of] refuge.
Please grant your blessing that my mind may move toward the Dharma.
Please grant your blessing that I may move toward the path of Dharma.
Please grant your blessing that obstacles to the Dharma will not arise.
Please grant your blessing that I may stop all wrong views, from lack of faith in the virtuous friend up to the two types of self-grasping.
Please grant your blessing that I may generate in my mental continuum all the realizations, from proper reliance upon the virtuous friend to death and impermanence, cause and effect of karma, renunciation, bodhichitta, the exalted wisdom realizing selflessness, and so forth, and may I never generate wrong views.
Please grant your blessing that I may generate the direct realization of the profound two stages of the path.

Make this request from the depth of your heart.

From the OM at the crown of the guru, limitless white light rays and nectar arise and enter through the crown of my head. My whole body is filled, and all the sickness, harm from spirits, negative karma, and obscurations and their imprints that I have accumulated with my body since beginningless lives are cleansed and purified. I receive the vase empowerment and receive the potential to attain the vajra body and the emanation body.

From the AH at the throat of the guru, limitless red light rays and nectar arise and enter through my throat. My whole body is filled, and all the sickness, harm from spirits, negative karma, and obscuration and their imprints that I have accumulated with my speech since beginningless lives are cleansed and purified. I receive the secret empowerment and receive the potential to attain the vajra speech and the enjoyment body.

From the HUM at the heart of the guru, limitless blue light rays and nectar arise and enter through my heart. My whole body is filled, and all the sickness, harm from spirits, negative karma, and obscuration and their imprints that I have accumulated with my mind since beginningless lives are cleansed and purified. I receive the exalted-wisdom empowerment and receive the potential to attain the vajra mind and the truth body.

Once again, from the three seed syllables at the three places of the guru, limitless white, red, and blue light rays and nectars arise and enter through the crown of my head, throat, and heart. My whole body is filled, and all the sickness, harm from spirits, negative karma, and obscuration and their imprints that I have accumulated with my body, speech, and mind since beginningless lives are cleansed and purified. I receive the fourth empowerment, my body, speech, and mind become inseparable from the three secrets, and I attain the good fortune to be able to attain the state of union of Vajradhara.

Then, make the request:

"My glorious and precious root guru, please sit on the lotus seat at my heart..." and so forth.

Due to this my guru is delighted and comes to sit on the crown of my head.

He melts into bodhichitta, descends through my central channel, and dissolves into the indestructible drop at my heart. My body, speech, and mind become inseparable from the body, speech, and mind of my guru.

Imagine:

My very subtle wind and mind become the nature of the body, speech, and mind of my guru.

Then to finish:

By this virtue may I quickly
Attain the state of the glorious guru
Then lead each living being
Without exception to that state.

Or make extensive prayers such as:

"In all my lives..."

Thus I have explained the extensive profound path of guru yoga.

THE ACTUAL SESSION

This section has five parts:

1. THE STAGE OF BLESSING THE SELF
2. THE STAGE OF THE VARIEGATED VAJRA
3. THE STAGE OF FILLING THE JEWEL
4. THE STAGE OF DZALANDHARA
5. THE STAGE OF INCONCEIVABILITY

The first part has two parts:

1. BLESSING THE SELF WITH SEED
2. BLESSING THE SELF WITHOUT SEED

[BLESSING THE SELF WITH SEED]

Follow the previous explanation as a preliminary and meditate on oneself as Heruka with one face and two hands. Sitting in the vajra posture, place your hands just below your navel [in the mudra of] meditative equipoise, spine straight, shoulders even, neck a little tilted [forward], and your eyes directed at the tip of the nose. In this way maintain the seven-point posture of Vairochana.

Directly in the center of your body, a little closer to your spine, is the central channel the width of a wheat stalk, possessing the following four qualities: red and oily like liquid resin, clear and luminous like a sesame oil lamp, straight and true like the trunk of a plantain tree, and soft and flexible like the petals of a lotus. Furthermore, visualize it as light blue on the outside with the [red] inside clearly visible. In this way it continues from the crown to the point between the eyebrows in a slight bend. The lower tip ends at the hole at the tip of the jewel; visualize them clearly. To the right is the red *roma* channel, and to the left is the white *kyangma* channel. Visualize clearly how both are connected to the central channel from the crown under the skull upon the brain to the point between the eye brows. The right and left channels wrap twice around [the central channel] and overlap to form knots. From the space between these knots come the channel wheels from the right and left channels, which constrict the central channel.

At the crown is the wheel of great bliss from which comes four channels in the four directions. Each one branches into two, making eight. Each one of those branches into two, making sixteen. From each of the sixteen [channels] come two, thereby forming thirty-two. Visualize clearly all the channel petals as multicolored, with the outer shape round like the spokes of an umbrella and the inner shape triangular. In the same way, at the throat just behind the Adam's apple, the right and left channels wrap around the central channel twice, forming two knots. Here, at the wheel of enjoyment at the throat are four channel petals; from these come eight, and from these sixteen. The channel petals are red, their shape is round, and the spokes are like an umbrella pointing upward. Imagine clearly these two channels pointing up and down as method and wisdom.

Then between the two breasts near the spine the central channel is constricted by three knots each. From these come eight channel petals, white in color and round in shape like an umbrella facing downward. At the navel the right and left channels constrict the central channel by forming two knots each. From between them come the first four channel petals of the navel. From them come eight, from them sixteen, from them four [making sixty-four] or from them come two each, and then two each again making sixty-four. The channel petals are of various colors, round in shape, and stretch upward like the spokes of an umbrella, the inner shape being triangular. Establish clearly the central channel and the channel petals. In the same way, at the secret place are channel knots and thirty-two channel petals. In the center of the jewel there are eight channel petals. In this way visualize [all the channels] very clearly.

Cleansing the Channels

Imagine the indestructible red and white drop at the heart radiates rays of light and moves up through the path of the central channel to the throat and up to the channel wheel at the crown, clearing all the channels with light. From there it returns to the heart and down to the navel, cleansing and purifying all the channels, then [returns] to the center of the heart channel wheel, where it abides as a drop, white on the top and red at the bottom, the size of a small pea and radiating rays of light.

In the center of that is an extremely subtle letter HUM, white and red like a pearl smeared with *sindhura* powder. The nada has three curves, the upper part is red, and the lower part is a little white and is a hundred times finer than if written by the tip of a hair; imagine this radiates limitless rays of light.

Blessing the Self without Seed

Begin by completing the gross and subtle meditation of the generation stage, and then gather everything into the clear light and visualize that you arise in the body of Heruka with one face and two hands as before. Expel the winds from the right to the left and the left to the right three times each, and then exhale equally three times through both the right and the left. After this nine-round breathing, visualize clearly the three channels and the six channel wheels as before. Then in the center of the channel wheel at the heart, visualize the [indestructible] red and white drop the size of a small pea with the two halves joined. In the center is the three-curved nada, red at the top and a little white at the bottom, with an extremely fine red tip. Its nature is hot to the touch, and from it arises a wind radiating five-colored light rays. Do not imagine that you are looking at it from outside, but meditate as if your mind had entered into the [nada].

Once Gaining Stability, How to Engage in Vajra Recitation

From the heart the five-colored light rays arise while making the sound HUM and go to the center of the channel wheel at the throat. While making the sound OM, they again return. While making the sound AH, they abide in the indestructible drop. Do this vajra recitation three times.

As before imagine [this time] they go all the way to the crown channel wheel, and again make the three recitations as before. Then the winds arise from the indestructible drop while making the sound HUM and go to the upper opening [of the central channel between the eyebrows]. They return from the upper opening while making the sound OM and enter the central channel and dissolve into the short A[90] at the indestructible drop, and while abiding they make the sound AH. The vajra recitation is the recitation of wind, and you should think that the winds and mantra are inseparable. By training in this single-pointedly, the winds will enter, abide, and dissolve into the central channel.

The definite sign that the winds have entered the central channel is that the movement of breath is of equal force through both nostrils. The sign that the winds are abiding [in the central channel] is that the wind moving through the nostrils becomes more and more subtle and finally stops. The sign that it has dissolved is [as follows]: When the earth wind dissolves into water, there is the mirage appearance. When the water wind dissolves into fire, there is the smoke appearance. When the fire wind dissolves into wind, there is the fireflies appearance. When the wind [begins to] dissolve into the [mind of] appearance, there is the vision like a blazing candle flame. When that wind [fully] dissolves, there is the vision of white appearance, empty like an autumn sky pervaded by white moonlight. At that time, cultivate the divine pride of having attained the vajra body. When that wind dissolves into the mind of increase, at that point there is an appearance of red increase like a pure autumn sky pervaded by sunlight. At that time, cultivate the divine pride of having attained the vajra speech. That wind dissolves into the mind of black near-attainment. At that point, there is an appearance of black near-attainment like a pure autumn sky pervaded by the thick blackness of night. At the same time, cultivate the divine pride of having attained the vajra mind. When the

90. Previously the Panchen Lama said there was a letter HUM at the heart, but now he is saying there is a short A, as in inner-heat meditation. This is perhaps because at this stage—blessing the self without seed—one visualizes merely the nada and not the letter HUM. While the nada is a three-curved squiggle atop the letter HUM, the short A is merely a vertical line; therefore, there are some similarities in their shapes.

[mind of black] near-attainment dissolves into the clear light, there arises an appearance like the sky at dawn, free from the three factors of white [appearance], red [increase], and black [near-attainment]. All dualistic appearances completely subside into the clear light, and you remain in meditative equipoise.

Then, with stable visualization at the heart, from the nada a flame blazes throughout all the channels, and the jasminelike bodhichitta descends. As it [descends] from the crown to the throat, there is joy; from the throat to the heart, supreme joy; from the heart to the navel, extraordinary joy; and from the navel to the tip of the jewel, abide in the experience of simultaneously born joy. Maintain the divine pride of the exalted wisdom of inseparable bliss and emptiness, which is the definitive emptiness held by the blissful awareness that realizes there is not even an atom of inherent existence in all phenomena of samsara and nirvana.

Again the [bodhichitta] arrives at the navel from the tip of the jewel and there is joy of reverse order; from the navel to the heart, supreme joy; from the heart to the throat, extraordinary joy; and from the throat to the crown, the simultaneously born bliss of reverse order. By inducing four joys [in reverse order], a superior joy to the previous four joys is experienced, and the four joys and the four empties are experienced as inseparable as they are generated in your mental continuum.

The Stage of the Variegated Vajra

This has two parts:

1. The Variegated Vajra with Seed
2. The Variegated Vajra without Seed

[the Variegated Vajra with Seed]

Perform the nine-round breathing technique and the seven essential postures of the body as before. Complete the recitation of the gross and subtle generation stage, collect [all phenomena into emptiness], then meditate on yourself as Heruka with one face and two hands together with the Mother Vajravarahi, who holds a curved knife and skull cup, with her legs wrapped around your waist as the Father, and abide in embrace. Establish clearly the three channels and the six chakras. The lower end of the central channel protrudes slightly beyond the tip of the jewel; the outer aspect is in the shape and aspect of the vajra [penis], and the inner shape is of a blue five-pronged vajra with its central spoke being the central channel the size of a small wheat straw.

The outer shape of the Mother's secret place is in the shape of a bhaga [vagina]. The inner shape is that of a three-petaled lotus. In the center of the corolla is a hole where the lower end of the Mother's central channel inserts into the lower end of your central channel. Where the two ends meet inside your own central channel, visualize a pink, one-pronged vajra facing upward. At its tip, or at its center, is HUM, either pink or white with a red luster. Then the indestructible drop at the heart rolls down the central channel to the tip [of the vajra] and dissolves into the letter HUM at its center. Your mind then enters into the nada of the letter HUM; place your mind in meditative stabilization. Then when you attain stability on that, the vajra and the seed [letter HUM] dissolve into the red and white drop, which then rises up through the central channel and comes to rest at the channel wheel at the heart.

[THE VARIEGATED VAJRA WITHOUT SEED]

As before, meditate on yourself as Heruka Father and Mother and establish clearly the three channels and the six channel wheels. At the upper end of the central channel where it ends between the eyebrows it is like a hollow reed; in it imagine there is a single-pronged, pink vajra, half inside the channel and half outside the channel. From the heart the indestructible drop rolls up through the central channel to the tip of the pink single-pronged vajra where the red part of the drop itself transforms into the aspect of a sun mandala blazing with light. Upon that, the white part of the drop transforms into the aspect of a white moon mandala, full and cool. In its center, meditate on a blue drop merely the size of a mustard seed radiating light, the nature of the lord of the lineage Akshobya. Visualize in front of that is a white drop, the nature of Vairochana; to the right, a yellow drop, the nature of Ratnasambhava; behind, a red drop, the nature of Amitabha; and to the left, a green drop, the nature of Amoghasiddhi. They are all only the size of small mustard seeds. Meditate until it is as though you can touch and see them. Then the drops in the four directions dissolve into the central drop. The central drop dissolves into the sun, moon, and vajra, and then transforms into a red and white drop merely the size of a mustard seed. Imagine it then rolls down the pathway of the central channel and abides in the center of the channel wheel at your heart. Then meditate on it single-pointedly until you attain clarity. The winds will then enter, abide, and dissolve as explained earlier.

The Stage of Filling the Jewel

This has four parts:

1. Action Mudra
2. Wisdom Mudra
3. Dharma Mudra
4. Mahamudra

[Action Mudra]

As before, cleanse the winds, the vital points of the body, and so forth. Complete the recitation of the self-generation with yourself as Heruka, complete with faces and arms[91] or one face and two arms. Generate the action mudra as Vajravarahi, possessing all the characteristics, and meditate that you enter into embrace. Establish clearly and completely the three channels and the six channel wheels. The Father's secret place is in the aspect of a blue five-pronged vajra, with the central channel merely the size of a wheat straw, with a hollow opening in the center, the nature of a spoke.

The Mother's secret place is in the aspect of a red three-petaled lotus, with anthers and a hole in its center, from which the central channel descends four finger widths. It is the width of merely a wheat straw. The

---

91. This means with four faces and twelve arms.

lower end of [the Mother's central channel, called] "crow face," meets with the lower end of your central channel. From within the Mother's central channel, the downward-voiding wind descends, and a very smooth wind, like smoke, enters your central channel through the hole at your vajra. This reaches the channel wheel at your navel and causes the *tummo* fire to blaze like bellows blowing on a blazing ember of steel as wind moves forcefully. This wind from below causes the fire to blaze even bigger, and as it burns it possesses the three characteristics of redness, clarity, and softness as it blazes upward throughout all the channels, and in particular, the flames cause the white bodhichitta in the aspect of a white letter HAM at your crown to melt. As it descends from your crown to your throat, you experience joy; as it descends from your throat to your heart, you experience supreme joy; as it descends from your heart to your navel, you experience extraordinary joy; and as it descends from your navel to the tip of your secret place, you experience simultaneously born bliss.

Then from your own secret place, the downward-voiding wind leaves your vajra path like smoke and enters the Mother's secret place. Moving upward it meets the tummo fire at her navel, causing it to blaze greatly, and melting the red bodhichitta, she experiences the four joys. When [the red bodhichitta] arrives [at the tip of the secret place], it enters the vajra path, and the red and white bodhichittas coalesce; visualize that your mind enters into that, and place your mind in meditative equipoise [on that red and white drop]. Meditate that the exalted wisdom of bliss and emptiness has been generated in your mental continuum, and in dependence upon this, your winds will enter, abide, and dissolve into the central channel; then engage in virtuous practice.

[WISDOM MUDRA]

There are no special differences in the action mudra and the wisdom mudra except that [the wisdom mudra] is visualized and [the action mudra] is real; everything else is as before.

[Dharma Mudra]

In the center of your secret place, where the red and white drops have coalesced, these [red and white drops] transform into a pink, one-pronged vajra, round in the center with very fine and subtle tips. Place your mind single-pointedly upon this and meditate on the exalted wisdom of bliss and emptiness.

[Mahamudra]

While sustaining this visualization without any difference from the three previous stages, stabilize the mind single-pointedly upon the secret place, and in dependence upon this meditation generate an extraordinary bliss. With this bliss [apprehending] the object emptiness, make an effort to penetrate the vital points of meditation and generate the exalted wisdom of inseparable bliss and emptiness.

The Stage of Dzalandhara

Do the preliminary of vital points of the body as before. With the divine pride of Heruka, establish clearly the three channels and six channel wheels. At your crown in the center of the wheel of great bliss is a moon mandala, and upon this is a white letter HAM hanging upside down. In the center of your heart channel wheel is a moon mandala from which a white letter HUM hangs upside down. In the four directions of the petals of the channel wheel are the four letters LAM, MAM, PAM, and TAM standing upright. Their colors are blue, yellow, red, and green [respectively]; imagine they are radiating light. In the center of your navel channel wheel inside the central channel is the phenomena source, white on the outside and red inside. In the center of that, the nature of Akshobya is a blue drop. In front, the nature of Vairochana is a white drop. To the right, the nature of Ratnasambhava is a yellow drop. Behind, the nature of Amitabha is a red drop. To the left, the nature of Amoghasiddhi is a green drop. They are the nature of the five lineages and the size of mustard seeds. This is the special object of meditation for blazing the tummo fire. Draw the wind from above downward and pull the wind from below upward, and bring them into embrace holding the vase breath. Imagine your mind has entered into the drops and hold it there. From the drop at the secret place [inside the phenomena source] the tummo fire blazes and moves up the path of the central channel. When it reaches the heart, it burns the five drops at the heart, and the bodhichitta drips onto the tummo fire. Then again the fire blazes, moving up the central channel reaching the white HAM at the crown and causing it to melt, and nectar falls like a string descending upon the tummo fire, whereby the pouring of nectar causes the fire to die down a little. Again it blazes bigger and ascends the path of the central channel. It arises from your right nostril, going out to all the buddhas, bodhisattvas, heroes, and dakinis in the ten directions, and enters through their nostrils and draws the nectar of exalted wisdom from their hearts, leaves their nostrils, and enters into your left nostril reviving the HAM at your crown. Then it revives the wheel of enjoyment [at the throat], then restores the burnt seed syllables at your heart and dissolves into the drops at your navel. Thus again and again meditate on the blazing and dripping, and in dependence upon that, generate in your mental continuum the exalted wisdom of inseparable bliss and emptiness.

The Stage of Inconceivability

After sustaining virtuous practices of the fourth stage you will see the signs of spontaneously accomplishing their meaning.

At dawn time when the sky is completely pure, rely upon the outer and inner conditions,[92] and directly realize the meaning of simultaneously born meaning [clear light] of emptiness with your mind placed in meditative equipoise on the exalted wisdom of great bliss. Subsequently rising from that spontaneous nature of meaning [clear light], the very subtle uncontaminated wind and mind will manifest directly as the body of great bliss of union adorned with all the marks and signs that one has abandoned [all faults] and realized [all good qualities].[93]

92. The outer condition is an action mudra; the inner condition is meditation on the channels, winds, and drops in conjunction with the two concentrations.
93. This is the illusory body.

Dispelling Obstacles of the Five Stages

Dispelling Mental Excitement

In the center of the red and white drop inside the central channel at the heart, [imagine] the letter HUM is very heavy, and meditate that your [mind] has sunk into the center of that drop. If that does not dispel [excitement], meditate that the HUM is made of iron and is very heavy and that [your mind] sinks into the drop and is impeded from escaping.

Dispelling Mental Sinking

From the letter HUM light rays shine clearly, radiating out and illuminating and clarifying all of the channels. They are filled with light like a lamp inside a crystal vase, which is illuminated inside and out.

Dispelling the Obstacles of the Channels

Imagine from the letter HUM light rays radiate, filling the inside of all the channels, opening the blocked, straightening the crooked, smoothing the rough, and stretching the bent, and all the pains and so forth of the channels are pacified.

Dispelling the Obstacles of the Winds

Imagine that light rays radiate from the letter HUM and the inside of all the channels are filled with blue rays of light in the aspect of smoke, which radiate from the letter HUM in the form of iron hooks that draw the winds inward and dissolve into the letter HUM. Generate an extraordinary exalted wisdom of bliss and emptiness in your mental continuum, and imagine that all illness is cleansed.

Developing the Enhancement of Bliss

At the center of your heart channel wheel is the letter HUM. Visualize clearly its tip as a flame with these three characteristics: bright red, hot and blazing, and flexible and bent. From the tongue of the flame, red light radiates. All of the channels are filled with white bodhichitta like stars. These are melted by the flames and dissolve into the nada of the HUM, like water descending and flowing through irrigation channels into ponds or like putting wood on a blazing flame that blazes even bigger. The jasminelike bodhichitta at the crown melts and descends through the path of the central channel and dissolves into the nada of the letter HUM together with the *tsetrak*. Imagine that you generate in your mental continuum unbearable great bliss as if you were going to faint.

Instructions on the Second Stage

Variegated Vajra with Seed

If the Obstacle of Dripping [Bodhichitta] Arises

Sit with your legs in the vajra posture. Take the tips of both thumbs and suppress the channel at the [base] of the ring fingers, make a fist and cross them at your heart while pressing down on your two breasts and draw your stomach in toward your spine. Reverse the eyes upward. As for the visualization, from your crown, light rays radiate in the aspect of two webs that descend through your central channel. At the lower end is a blue letter HUM with its head pointing upward, and these two webs arrive one in front of the other. At the secret place is the single-pronged pink vajra with seed. The two tips hook the shabkyu and the nada, pulling them upward. Then, like a blacksmith who extracts a hot piece of metal with a pair of tongs, imagine that the variegated vajra with seed is drawn upward inside the central channel. With your speech recite the long HUM twenty-one times: three times up the center of the jewel channel wheel, three times to the secret place, three times to the navel, three times to the heart, three times to the throat, and three times to the crown. When you [recite it three more times to make] twenty-one, imagine it dissolves into the channel wheel at the crown. From there imagine the white drop is spread out throughout all the channels.

Colophon

This explicit commentary is on the profound path of the two stages
Of glorious Heruka Chakrasamvara,
The sole jewel of all worlds,
The powerful being victorious in battle.

For the sake of increasing the profound yoga,
I, Losang Chökyi Gyaltsen,
Have arranged this pure white collection
For the sake of liberating all beings from samsara.

*Thus I have composed an explanatory commentary of the profound five stages in
the tradition of Wangchuk Tibul Shab [the powerful Ghantapa Shab], the greatest of the great secrets from the ear-to-ear lineage. The great being protecting the
land, named Ul Gyal Norbu, requested this text. The rough draft of these notes was
prepared, and I myself checked them again and made any necessary corrections.*

*This profound commentary on the highest mantra [should not be seen] unless one
has received purely the four empowerments; to others this should not even be shown.
Also, each year there cannot be more than two copies made. If you exceed more
than that the guardians and dharma protectors possessing power and ability will
annihilate you with their wrath.*

The nine moods of the youthful sapphire, the sphere of reality,
In the dance of embrace with the lightning[like] goddess of great bliss,
Constantly frolicking in the center of an indestructible tent,
Kye, [this] quickly bestows union endowed with love.

In dependence upon the ship—the oral instructions of Manjushri,
The powerful captain—Losang Dorje Chang—leads one
To the wish-fulfilling jewel that [reveals] the tantra's hidden meaning,
Bestowing the fortunate upon the supremely fortunate.

Arisen from the source of ten million supreme siddhas of India and
Tibet,

The fortunate easily enter the path to Kachö[94] and
Quickly and even more quickly accomplish union;
Eh Ma, the fortune of one who finds such a method.

In this case the unmistaken, wholly unmistaken companion who
Appears unattached, completely unattached to the glory of existence and
Without cherishing, without cherishing in the slightest the lesser [path
    of] peace and happiness,
[Remains] unmoving, wholly unmoving from persevering in this path.

The merit of the trader from Rongbo called Kelsang
Who sponsored the publication of this tantra is perfectly pure.
Therefore, without question his merit will increase
And become vast in the jewel heart of the one who makes effort.

May he himself, myself, and all living beings
Realize that being in the ocean of existence is without meaning and
With the swift horse of great waves in the jeweled mind
Enter into the ripening and liberating path of the glorious body
    mandala.

Emanating a mandala that is the basis of death, bardo, and rebirth
By the contrived and uncontrived paths of the three bodies,
And by purifying the resultant nature of the stable and moving,
May I be quickly liberated in the pure and limitless mandala.

The Dharma Lord who is the collection of heroes and yoginis at the
    three places,
Has given permission to publish this.
Thus may I quickly attain such power in my mind as a practitioner,
And may it be the constant outer, inner, and secret helper.

Thus this [completes] the very profound commentary on the profound five stages
of the Bhagawan Chakrasamvara in the tradition of Mahasiddha Ghantapa. By

94. Kachö is the pure land of Heruka and Vajrayogini.

composing these dedication verses of this path, may it become a cause to multiply the virtues of the benefactor, Kelsang the trader from Rongbo, who is making uninterrupted effort in the yoga of this path. This was prepared by Pabongkha Dechen Nyingpo who is [merely] a reflection of a yogi of this path while he was staying in the isolated place Tashi Chöling in the Earth Bird Year [1888]. This has descended from the source of the speech of Panchen Suddhi Vajra at Tashi Lhunpo. Once again [Kyabje Trijang Dorje Chang] took the previous publication from Tashi Chöling and published this text during Losar in the Western year 1970.

The method of accomplishment—glorious Heruka,
Binds all things stable and moving with simultaneous great bliss.
This commentary elucidates the profound path of the second stage of
    the body mandala
As set forth in the tradition of the supreme siddha Ghantapa Shab.

Through the power of the beautiful, youthful moon of joy of
Printing this and the inexhaustible merit of giving Dharma,
May the stainless teachings of this excellent tradition of the
Able One and the Venerable Gentle Protector pervade this world.

May all living beings who have made any donation to this publication
Travel to the end of this excellent ripening and liberating path
Of Heruka Chakrasamvara and the three principal paths,
And accomplish the union of the bhagawan hero.

These verses of dedication were composed by Kyabje Yongzin Trijang Dorje Chang the Great.
Carved by the publisher Penpa Norbu and printed at Do Se Mel Li Ru.[95]

---

95. According to Gen Lobsang Choephel, this is a printing house in India.

Ngulchu Dharmabhadra's
Retreat Instructions

How to Engage in an Action-Permitting Retreat[96] of Heruka Five Deity, Entitled *Illuminating the Meaning of the Essential Letter*

NAMA SHRI CHAKRASAMVARAYA

I bow to the root and lineage gurus of the powerful four bodies, and
To the deity, Heruka Father and Mother.
I shall compose a brief retreat ritual on the profound meaning of
The outer mandala of the five deities of Ghantapa.

The method for performing an action-permitting retreat in dependence upon the sadhana of Heruka five deity, entitled *Source of Great Bliss,*[97] has four parts: (1) who can perform the retreat, (2) where to perform the retreat, (3) when to perform the retreat, and (4) how to perform the retreat.

Who Can Perform the Retreat

The practitioner who is suitable to perform the retreat is one who has trained his mental continuum in the common path, has obtained the four empowerments into this mandala, abides in the general and specific vows and commitments, and who, before undertaking the retreat, has removed all doubts concerning the meaning of the words of the sadhana. In this way, the practitioner must have made an effort to properly complete all of these [preliminaries].

---

96. An action-permitting retreat (Tib. *las rung*) is a retreat involving mantra recitation that permits you to engage in mandala actions such as self-initiation and image consecration. This is a more specific type of "close retreat." Whereas a close retreat brings you closer to the deity, not all close retreats are action-permitting retreats, but all action-permitting retreats are necessarily close retreats.
97. This is the sadhana of the First Panchen Lama. Yanchen Drupay Dorje based his work (included in this publication) upon this sadhana.

WHERE TO PERFORM THE RETREAT

Since it will be difficult for a beginning practitioner to endure such places as charnel grounds, the homes of evil female spirits,[98] and so forth, as taught in the tantras, it should be a place that has been previously blessed by a holy being, as well as one that is isolated and free from the disturbance of commotion. Such a place should not have any discordant conditions such as susceptibility to potential harm to your life by humans or nonhumans and should be a place where all favorable conditions are assembled, such as [clean] water, firewood, and so forth. It should be pleasant and a place that is under your own power and where resides a tantric assistant.[99]

WHEN TO PERFORM THE RETREAT

The period during the twelfth month of the Tibetan calendar, called Gyal Da,[100] and during the two tenth days of the waxing and waning moon are the auspicious times of this deity. However, beginning the retreat during any other month or day of the week that is good and agreeable would also not be inappropriate. It has been said that the first session should begin in the evening around eight o'clock.

HOW TO PERFORM THE RETREAT

This has three parts:

1. PREPARING FOR THE RETREAT
2. THE ACTUAL RETREAT
3. CONCLUDING THE RETREAT

---

98. The term for this is *mamos* (Tib. *ma mo*).

99. This is because if you are in a retreat house that is under someone else's control there is always the possibility that he or she may force you to leave before you have completed your retreat.

100. Gyal Da (Tib. *rgyal gyi zla*) is from the sixteenth day of the eleventh month to the fifteenth day of the twelfth month. The two "tenth days" are the tenth and the twenty-fifth, which are ten days after the new moon and the full moon respectively.

Preparing for the Retreat

A few days prior to your retreat, you should earnestly engage in the rituals for purifying [negative karma] and accumulating [virtuous karma]. In addition, you should assemble all the articles you will need for the preliminary [puja] and carefully study the texts concerning the retreat. Rise early in the morning on the first day of the retreat and sweep both the inside and outside of your house, burn excellent incense, and sprinkle the five nectars and cow substances.[101] Then, face south, or at least imagine that you are facing in that direction. Draw a variegated vajra upon which you should scatter flowers, arrange a cushion of jointed grass,[102] and lay out your cushion. On the south side of the retreat house, set out a picture or statue of the Deity Father and Mother facing you, as well as a volume of tantra and so forth to act as the three supreme supports. In front of these, within some type of torma box [arrange a torma] made from clean barley flour mixed with rice dough, peas, and white garlic. Mix these together into dough and blend the powder with nectar. Take [a mixture of] water, beer, milk, and melted butter, and shape it into a round torma made from clean pastry encircled with four small ball tormas,[103] coat these with [red] paint, and adorn them with a moon, sun, nada, and so forth. To the left of this is the torma to the general dakinis, which is round and painted[104] with white and red ornaments.[105] In front of this are the outer offerings for the self- and front-generations, with the two waters and the close enjoyment offerings set out in two rows; these two should be arranged beginning from the left of the object of the offerings. In front of you, beginning from the left [and going to the right], is a rosary made of

---

101. "Pa chung" (Tib. *ba byung*) consists of the five cow substances: milk, butter, yogurt, urine, and feces. These are prepared in pills by Tibetan monasteries in exile.
102. Tib. *rtsa dur ba*.
103. Tib. *bshos bu*.
104. Tib. *dba' bshos zlum po smug rtsi*.
105. In the Panchen Lama's sadhana that Ngulchu Dharmabhadra is commenting on, there is no preliminary torma. Usually there are three tormas: the central one is for the Father, Mother, and the four dakinis; the one to the left is for the mundane guests; and the one to the right (but not included in this commentary) would be a similar torma for the preliminary torma. In our sadhana the members of Zongkhar Chöde have added the preliminary torma to the sadhana. Therefore, for our purposes we need all three tormas.

either human bones or bodhi seeds. Near at hand, have a hand drum, bell, vajra, inner offering, grains for tossing, and an action vase with the proper substances, and, if you have them, a katvanga, Brahmin thread, skull cup, bone ornaments, and so forth. [In this way] assemble all the necessary [ritual] articles and put on clean clothes. Moreover you will need an obstacle-dispelling torma, fire container, gugal, and mustard seeds, and will need to set up a boundary marker together with an offering torma. Assemble all the offerings and tormas thus, and place them upon a raised platform.

Then having arranged your seat, go for refuge, generate bodhichitta, and arise as the instantaneous self-generation. Inside the vase on a sun mandala is a letter BAM, surrounded by the mantra rosary, from which light rays radiate. Going to the ten directions, they invoke the power, strength, ability, and blessings of all the buddhas, bodhisattvas, heroes, yoginis, dharma protectors, and guardians, all of whom are in the aspect of Kandharohi. Having dissolved into the mantra rosary and seed syllable, a stream of nectar descends and fills the vase, blessing and empowering it so that it is able to dispel obstructing spirits and impurities. While imagining this, recite the Kandharohi mantra. It is in this way that the secret water is accomplished. Then bless the inner offering, outer offering, and tormas according to the sadhana.

Obstacle-Dispelling Torma

Cleanse with:

OM KHANDAROHI HUM HUM PHAT

Purify with:

OM SÖBHAWA SHUDDHA SARWA DHARMA SÖBHAWA SHUDDHO HAM

Then bless with:

OM AKHAROMUKHAM SARWA DHARMANEN ADENUWATEN
NADO DA NAMA SARWA TATHAGATA AWOLIKETE OM
SAMBHARA SAMBHARA HUM (3x)

Then offer the torma three times and, as you complete each [mantra], one torma is offered each time, pacifying and cleansing the perimeter.

OM SARWA BIGNAM NAMA SARWA TATHAGATO BAYO BISHO
MUKE BE SARWA DEKANG UGATE PARANA IMAM GA GA NA
KHANG GRIHANA DAM BALINGTAYE SÖHA (3x)

Then:

OM SUMBHANI SUMBHA HUM HUM PHAT
OM GRIHANA GRIHANA HUM HUM PHAT
OM GRIHANA PAYA GRIHANA PAYA HUM HUM PHAT
OM ANAYA HO VIDYA RADZA HUM HUM PHAT

As you complete each recitation, offer one tinglo and one finger torma in combination as before, cleansing and pacifying wrathful [spirits].

Then [proclaim]:

You interfering spirits abiding in this place, please accept this torma I am offering you and be satisfied, pacify your harmful and vicious minds from now until I complete the retreat, and generate peaceful and benevolent minds, and return to your own places.

While saying this, send out the torma, make a vajra fist, play the instruments loudly, say the SUMBHANI and Kandharohi mantras wrathfully, burn gugal, sprinkle secret water, and toss mustard seeds.

Recite:

From the HUM at my heart light rays radiate, and instantaneously there arises a vajra ground, fence, tent, canopy, and mountain of fire.

Contemplate who will be allowed to enter the retreat house and make note of their names.

Putting on the Armor of Father and Mother for Protection

At his heart a moon seat is marked by a white OM AH, the nature of Vajrasattva. At his head, on a sun seat, is a yellow NAMA HI, the nature of Vairochana. At his crown, on a sun seat, is a red SOHA HU, the nature of Pamanarteshvara. At his two shoulders, on a sun seat, is a black BOKE HE, the nature of glorious Heruka. At his two eyes, on a sun seat, is an orange HUM HUM HO, the nature of Vajrasurya. At his forehead, on a sun seat, is a green PHAT HAM, the nature of Paramashawa.

At the Principal Mother's navel, on a sun seat, is a red OM BAM, the nature of Vajravarahi. At her heart, on a sun, is a blue HAM YAM, the nature of Yamani. At her throat, on a moon, is a white HRIM MOM, the nature of Mohani. At her head, on a sun, is a yellow HRIM HRIM, the nature of Sachalani. At her crown, on a sun, is a green HUM HUM, the nature of Samtrasani. At her forehead, on a sun seat, is a smoke-colored PHAT PHAT, the nature of Chandika.

Next, at the entranceway of the retreat house, generate the retreat boundary, and in front of it arrange an offering torma and bless it according to the sadhana.

The boundary marker is cleansed by Kandharohi and purified with SOBHAWA, and from the state of emptiness comes a lotus and moon upon which is the great King Birshudhaka,[106] with a blue-colored body, one face, and two hands, holding a sword. He is adorned with silks and jeweled ornaments, displayed in the manner of a king. At his crown is a [white] OM, at his throat a [red] AH, and at his heart a [blue] HUM. From the HUM at his heart, light rays radiate and invoke Birshudhaka and his retinue from their abode on the southern side of Mount Meru.

OM VAJRA SAMAYA DZA, DZA, HUM, BAM, HO

---

106. Tib. *phag pa'i kye po.*

They become nondual.

Through a hollow tube of light on his tongue, the great King Birshudhaka partakes of the essence of the torma.

OM MAHA RADZA BIRSHU DHAKA SAPARIWARA IDAM BALINGTA KA KA KHA HI KHA HI

Recite and offer three times.

OM MAHA RADZA BIRSHU DHAKA SAPARIWARA AHRGHAM . . . up to SHAPTA

Then offer praise with:

I prostrate to Birshudhaka,
The extremely powerful great hero,
Blue in color, holding a sword, and
Subjugating the host of evil spirits.[107]

Then request the fulfillment of wishes while tossing flowers.

Until I perfectly accomplish this retreat,
Pacify all inner and outer hindrances,
And perform your enlightened actions
To accomplish all favorable conditions.

Make abbreviated offerings.

The Actual Retreat

In the evening, the time when the dakinis gather, sit upon a comfortable

---

107. Tib. *grul bum*. According to Sarat Chandra Das's dictionary these are "a class of vampire-ghouls feeding in the cemeteries."

seat, with your body endowed with all the essential features.[108] With [at least] a contrived motivation, make requests to the lineage gurus, go for refuge and generate bodhichitta, arise as the instantaneous self-generation, then bless the inner offering and the offerings to the self-generation. And, if you have the inclination, stitch together the explanation from the commentary and do Vajrasattva meditation and recitation. Make offerings to the field of merit. Recite the SHUNYATA mantra, and dissolve all worlds and their beings into yourself and recite, "I as well dissolve into emptiness." This is the practice of "bringing death into the path of the truth body." Then do the practice of "bringing the intermediate state into the enjoyment body." Meditate on the protection circle, the four elements, and Mount Meru, and generate the supporting and supported mandalas from the five manifest enlightenments. This is the practice of "bringing rebirth into the path of the emanation body." Visualize this clearly in stages. Then bless the four places and the secret places of the Father and Mother, and by entering into embrace meditate on the corresponding purities. If you are inclined, you can put on the armor according to the previous explanation by merely using the mantras. Bless the three places of all the deities. Absorb the wisdom beings. Bestow the empowerment and seal [with the lords of the lineage]. Make the outer, inner, secret, and suchness offerings. Offer the mantras. If you have the time, you should say the eight lines of praise to the Father in Sanskrit.

Eight Lines of Praise to the Father

OM NAMO BHAGAWATE WIRE SHAYA HUM HUM PHAT

OM MAHA KÄLWA AHGNI SAMNI BHAYA HUM HUM PHAT

OM DZATA MUGUTRA KORTAYA HUM HUM PHAT

OM DHAMKHATRA KARA LOTRA BHIKHANA MUKAYA HUM
    HUM PHAT

OM SAHARA BHUNDZA BHASURAYA HUM HUM PHAT

OM PARASHUWA SHODHÄDA SHULA KHATAMGA DHARINE
    HUM HUM PHAT

---

108. Here, the "essential features" refer to the seven-point posture of Vairochana.

OM BHÄGADZINAM WARA DHARAYA HUM HUM PHAT

OM MAHA DHUMA ÄNDHAKARA WAWUKAYA HUM HUM PHAT

Eight Lines of Praise to the Mother

OM NAMO BHAGAWATI VAJRA VARAHI BAM HUM HUM PHAT

OM NAMO ARYA APARADZITE TRE LOKYA MATI BIYE SHÖRI
HUM HUM PHAT

OM NAMA SARWA BUTA BHAYA WAHI MAHA VAJRE HUM HUM
PHAT

OM NAMO VAJRA SANI ADZITE APARADZITE WASHAM KARA-
NITRA HUM HUM PHAT

OM NAMO BHRAMANI SHOKANI ROKANI KROTE KARALENI
HUM HUM PHAT

OM NAMA DRASANI MARANI PRABHE DANI PARADZAYE HUM
HUM PHAT

OM NAMO BIDZAYE DZAMBHANI TAMBHANI MOHANI HUM
HUM PHAT

OM NAMO VAJRA VARAHI MAHA YOGINI KAME SHÖRI KHAGE
HUM HUM PHAT

Offering of Praise

O Great and Glorious Hero Heruka,
Having control over your pure vajra;
To Vajravarahi and those
Powerful heroes and heroines
In the places, near places, fields,
Meeting places, and charnel grounds;
Who generate great attachment in the mind of your devotees,
To all of you respectfully I prostrate.

Next, meditate briefly on self-generation. Then bless the mala by reciting:

The mala transforms into the nature of vajra-speech.

The visualization [during mantra] recitation is as follows.

On a sun seat at the heart of each deity is a sun seat upon which is a letter HUM, surrounded by the mantra rosary being recited, arranged counterclockwise. From the letter HUM in the center, a host of mandala deities radiate out and accomplish the welfare of migrating beings. Once again they collect and dissolve into the letter HUM. By continuing in this manner—radiating and collecting—you accomplish all of the essential features of both the heap and commitment recitations. While maintaining that state, with the thumb and ring finger of the left hand, pull the beads of the mala as you recite [the mantra].

As for the number of recitations, for merely an action-permitting retreat, recite the essence mantras of both the Father and Mother one hundred thousand times each. As for the close-essence mantras, recite these as much as you can.[109] As for the retinue and wisdom-descending mantras, recite these ten thousand times each, and then perform the subsequent pacifying fire puja to the best of your ability. If you wish [to recite] the condensed wisdom-descending mantra, it is as follows:

OM HRIH HA HA HUM HUM PHAT OM TIKTRA MAHA KRODRA ABESHAYA HUM

This is taught to be valid and permissible. As for the visualization:

From the HUM at your heart, red hooklike light rays radiate and invoke all the buddhas, bodhisattvas, heroes, and yoginis in the aspect of Heruka Chakrasamvara five deities. Imagine they descend upon your body like a great rain and enter through all of your pores; they dissolve into you and become nondual. At the end of the recitation, imagine at the hearts of each of the lords of the lineage,[110] upon a moon cushion, a HUM surrounded by the hundred-syllable Heruka [Vajrasattva] mantra, circling counterclockwise, from which purifying nectar descends,

---

109. In most commentaries it says to recite each of the close-essence mantras ten thousand times.
110. These are the lords of the lineage that sit upon the crowns of each of the five deities.

fulfilling all excesses and omissions and stabilizing the blessing. At this point, according to the intention of Je Lama [Tsongkhapa], one should offer a torma. Do this in the same manner as one blesses the mundane and supramundane tormas.

[*Recite:*]

PHAIM

From the letter HUM at my heart, light rays radiate and invoke the directional protectors, field protectors, nagas, and so forth, together with their retinue, who abide in the eight charnel grounds in the aspect of the mandala of Heruka five deities, to the space before me.

Offering the Torma

From a HUM at the tongues of the deities arises a three-pronged vajra, and through tubes of light the size of only a grain of barley they partake of the essence of the torma.

OM VAJRA AH RA LI HO: DZA HUM BAM HO: VAJRA DAKINI SAMAYA TÖN TRISHAYA HO (3x)

This is the offering to the supramundane deities.

Outer Offerings

OM SARWA TATHAGATA AHRGHAM PRATITZA SÖHA
OM SARWA TATHAGATA PADÄM PRATITZA SÖHA
OM SARWA TATHAGATA PUPE PRATITZA SÖHA
OM SARWA TATHAGATA DHUPE PRATITZA SÖHA
OM SARWA TATHAGATA DIWE PRATITZA SÖHA
OM SARWA TATHAGATA GÄNDHE PRATITZA SÖHA
OM SARWA TATHAGATA NEWIDE PRATITZA SÖHA
OM SARWA TATHAGATA SHAPTA PRATITZA SÖHA

Inner Offering

OM HRIH HA HA HUM HUM PHAT, OM AH HUM
OM SARWA BUDDHA DAKINIYE VAJRA WARNARNIYE HUM
    HUM PHAT SÖHA, OM AH HUM
OM DAKINIYE HUM HUM PHAT, OM AH HUM
OM LAME HUM HUM PHAT, OM AH HUM
OM KHANDAROHI HUM HUM PHAT, OM AH HUM
OM RUPINIYE HUM HUM PHAT, OM AH HUM

Eight Lines of Praise to the Father

OM I prostrate to the Bhagawan, powerful lord of the heroes
    HUM HUM PHAT
OM To you with a light equal to the fire of the great eon
    HUM HUM PHAT
OM To you who possess an inexhaustible crown of hair
    HUM HUM PHAT
OM To you with a terrifying face and bared fangs HUM HUM PHAT
OM To you who have a thousand arms of blazing light
    HUM HUM PHAT
OM To you who hold an axe, a noose, a spear, and a katvanga
    HUM HUM PHAT
OM To you who wear a tiger-skin garment HUM HUM PHAT
OM I bow to you whose great smoke-colored body destroys all
    obstructions HUM HUM PHAT

Eight Lines of Praise to the Mother

OM I prostrate to the bhagawati Vajravarahi HUM HUM PHAT
OM To the powerful Arya Knowledge-Goddess, invincible in the three
    realms HUM HUM PHAT
OM To you who destroy with your great vajra the fear of all demons
    HUM HUM PHAT
OM To you whose eyes empower those who sit on the vajra seat not to
    be overcome by others HUM HUM PHAT

OM To you whose wrathful body of psychic heat can desiccate Brahma
   HUM HUM PHAT
OM To you who terrify and dry up demons and thus can vanquish other
   forces HUM HUM PHAT
OM To you who conquer all that makes us dull, excited, and confused
   HUM HUM PHAT
OM I bow to the consort Vajravarahi, the dakini who has the power of
   desire HUM HUM PHAT

Requesting the Fulfillment of Wishes

You who have destroyed equally the conceptions attached to samsara
   and peace,
And are endowed with the spacelike vision of all things,
O Protector, by the moisture of your great compassion and strong love,
May goddesses truly take me under their loving care.

Offering the Torma to the Mundane Dakas and Dakinis

The directional protectors, field protectors, nagas and so forth who abide
in the eight charnel grounds instantly enter into the clear light and arise
in the aspect of Heruka Father and Mother. From a HUM at their tongues
arises a three-pronged vajra, and through tubes of light the size of only a
grain of barley they partake of the essence of the torma.

OM KHA KHA, KHAHI KHAHI, SARWA YAKYA RAKYASA,
BHUTA, TRETA, PISHATSA, UNATA, APAMARA, VAJRA DAKA,
DAKI NÄDAYA, IMAM BALING GRIHANTU, SAMAYA RAKY-
ANTU, MAMA SARWA SIDDHI METRA YATZANTU, YATIPAM,
YATETAM, BHUDZATA, PIWATA, DZITRATA MATI TRAMATA,
MAMA SARWA KATAYA, SÄDSUKHAM BISHUDAYE, SAHAYEKA
BHAWÄNTU, HUM HUM PHAT PHAT SÖHA (2X)

Outer Offerings

OM AHRGHAM PRATITZA SÖHA

OM PADÄM PRATITZA SÖHA
OM VAJRA PUPE AH HUM SÖHA
OM VAJRA DHUPE AH HUM SÖHA
OM VAJRA DIWE AH HUM SÖHA
OM VAJRA GÄNDHE AH HUM SÖHA
OM VAJRA NEWIDE AH HUM SÖHA
OM VAJRA SHAPTA AH HUM SÖHA

Inner Offering

To the mouths of the directional guardians, regional guardians, nagas, and so forth, OM AH HUM.

Requests

For the sake of protecting the teachings
And accomplishing the welfare of sentient beings,
You have taken oaths and heart commitments.
Great and glorious agents swift as the mind,
With terrifying bodies and inexhaustible wrath,
Who subdue the vicious and destroy those on the dark side,
Who bestow results to the practice of yoga,
With inconceivable strength, power, and blessing,
To the eight harm-givers and so forth I prostrate.
I request your wives, children, and servants
To bestow the kindness of all attainments.

If you want to make the torma offering shorter, do the first part in the same way as above up to the inner offering to the deity, then:

OM SARWA TATHAGATA, OM AH HUM

Respectfully I prostrate to the lotus feet of
The supreme guru-deity Heruka,
The always loving, venerable Mother,
And to the powerful heroes and heroines.

Then make request for your wishes:

To the collection of mandala deities in all the directions, please pacify the unfavorable circumstances, obstacles, and hindrances of myself and every living being, and please bestow your blessings to accomplish all our wishes and collect all excellent favorable conditions.

Then request actions from the worldly beings:

Directional protectors, regional protectors, nagas, and so forth,
Please accept this cloud of torma offerings
That I, the yogi, and my retinue may
Receive all the attainments we desire.

OM VAJRA MU

The mundane beings return to their own places.

OM YOGA SHUDDHA SARWA DHARMA YOGA SHUDDHO HAM

Then say:

The deities and mandala in front dissolve into me.

In the evening session make the dedication prayers and auspicious prayers. During the other three sessions, if you offer a torma, continue on from the point of sending away the guests. If you don't make a torma offering, then at the end of the [mantra] recitation recite the dissolution:

From the HUM at my heart light rays radiate, the supporting mandala dissolves into the retinue; the retinue dissolves into the four faces; I as Father and Mother dissolve into the letter HUM; the HUM completely transforms and I appear clearly as Heruka with my three places marked by OM AH HUM.

Then recite from "Requesting the Fulfillment of Wishes," that states,

"You who have destroyed equally the conceptions attached to samsara and peace..." onward through the dedication prayers.

As for the practice of sleeping yoga, collect everything into the letter HUM in your heart as done during the dissolution in the sadhana; the HUM dissolves sequentially from below up to the nada; the nada also dissolves into unobservable inseparable bliss and emptiness; imagine that you have manifested the truth body, and then go to sleep.

As for the yoga of arising at dawn the next morning, imagine the yoginis are singing songs and playing damarus by which you are stirred from sleep. Recite, "From the state of emptiness, I arise clearly as Heruka with my three places marked by OM AH HUM." After arising you should do as just explained from the contrived motivation up to the dedication prayers. As for the [other] morning session, the afternoon session, and the evening session, if you wish to make them a little shorter, it is permissible to leave aside the request to the lineage gurus, the Vajrasattva meditation and recitation, putting on the armor, and the eight lines of praise. It is also permissible to set aside the torma offerings and the auspicious prayers except for the last session. As this outline is already very short, it is not permissible to make it any shorter.

During the session breaks, you must also see your body as the deity body and your speech as proclamations of mantra, and without allowing your mind to waver from bliss and emptiness, engage in the yoga of daily actions. Bless your food and drink as the inner offering. Imagine the HUM at your heart is the nature of all the deities and make offerings to them, thinking that it is the yoga of enjoying food and drink.

[As for the yoga of washing], imagine that light rays radiate from your heart and invoke washing goddesses who hold vases and bestow the empowerment so that all harm from spirits, sickness, negative karma, and obscurations is purified and you generate bliss and emptiness and wash your hands and rinse your mouth. This is the yoga of washing.

Whatever is not clear here such as the preparation, the actual retreat, and how to end it should be learned from other similar notes on this retreat. Also, by studying the commentaries on the generation stage you should be able to figure it out. You should avoid superstitions of being high and low, being timid and arrogant, and being hopeful and fearful, and dispense with such doubts. With great joy and happiness you should make effort continuously like a river.

How to Conclude the Retreat

Once you have perfectly completed the counting retreat in this way, arrange fresh tormas and earnestly perform the thanking offerings, praises, fulfilling offerings, tsok offering, subsequent pacifying burnt offering, hundred-syllable mantra, requesting forbearance, dedication verses, and auspicious prayers. Then you should end the retreat in the morning session, arrange a torma offering in front of the boundary marker, and bless it according to the text. Recite, "From the tongue of the great King Birshudhaka come tubes of light . . ." and "I prostrate to the great King Birshudhaka. . . ." Complete it as done before. [See below.]

Tubes of light from the tongue of the great King Birshudhaka partake of the essence of the torma.

OM MAHA RADZA BIRSHU DHAKA SAPARIWARA IDAM BAL-INGTA KA KA KHA HI KHA HI

Recite three times.

OM MAHA RADZA BIRSHU DHAKA SAPARIWARA ARGHAM . . . up to SHAPTA

Then:

I prostrate to the great King Birshudhaka,
The extremely powerful great hero,
Blue in color, holding a sword, and
Subjugating the host of evil spirits.

While tossing flowers, request the fulfillment of wishes and recite:

Until I perfectly accomplish this retreat,
Pacify all inner and outer hindrances
And perform your enlightened actions
To accomplish all favorable conditions.[111]

Recite the hundred-syllable mantra to purify excesses and omissions, then recite the verse, "Whatever was degenerate or not found…" and request forbearance.

OM

The great King Birshudhaka and his retinue,
Famous for assisting in enlightened actions,
Return to your own place and
Come here again when you are needed.

VAJRA MU

The wisdom beings return to their own abodes and the commitment beings dissolve into me.

Then, take the old offerings and tormas that have been blessed, and either partake of them yourself or pour them in some [large body of] water [such as a lake or a river]. After this the accomplished substances that are inside and outside should be gradually dispersed.

Colophon

Without being discouraged for three countless great eons,
In one life of this degenerate age you bestow
The supreme state of the three bodies through

---

111. It seems to me that this should say,

> Now that I have completed the retreat,
> Please continue to pacify all inner and outer hindrances
> And perform your enlightened actions
> To accomplish all favorable conditions.

This most profound of the 220 million highest yoga tantras.[112]
The meaning of the root and the
Essence of explanatory tantras of Chakrasamvara that
Were condensed by Mahasiddha Ghantapa,
Losang Drakpa [Tsongkhapa], and Dharmabhadra[113]
Is like the essence of nectar of the good scriptures.

In dependence upon these [masters] I have composed the method
For engaging in the action-permitting retreat of
The teaching of many holy siddhas and scholars.

Whatever virtue there is from this clear explanation,
May I accomplish the state of union.

Thus, herein have I explained the method for undertaking the action-permitting retreat of Heruka five deity, entitled *Illuminating the Meaning of the Essential Letter*. It was composed by the Shakya[114] monk Dharmabhadra during the auspicious time of the first day of the waxing moon of the Rabbit Year[115] in Ngulchu Cave.

112. Since usually there are said to be 160 million mother tantras, it is unclear as to why this reads 220.
113. Clearly this poem was composed by Yangchen Drupay Dorje since it refers to Ngulchu Dharmabhadra.
114. This refers to Ngulchu Dharmabhadra being a Buddhist monk following Shakyamuni, not the Sakya lineage of Tibetan Buddhism.
115. There seems to be an editing error in the Tibetan text. The year and the month are unclear.

PART 2

Ritual Texts

The Lamp Illuminating the Condensed Essence of Great Bliss

RESTRICTED MATERIAL

This may be read only by those who have received a highest-yoga tantra empowerment.

In order to practice this material, one must have received the complete empowerment into the five deity Mandala of Heruka Chakrasamvara of Maha-siddha Ghantapa, according to the lineage of Lama Tsongkhapa.

This sadhana was composed by Yanchen Drupay Dorje, the heart-disciple of Ngulchu Dharmabhadra and his successor as the lineage holder for the Ganden oral lineage. This sadhana is based on the more extensive Heruka five deity sadhana by the First Panchen Lama, Losang Chökyi Gyaltsen. Yangchen Drupay Dorje, fearing it was too long for today's lazy and distracted practitioners, extracted some sections to make the sadhana more manageable.

The version you have before you now is from Zongkhar Chöde Monastery, now relocated in India, and they have taken the liberty to add the following sections: blessing the vajra and bell, mandala, Vajrasattva, and preliminary torma; as well as expanding some of the notes interspersed throughout the sadhana.

NAMO GURU SHRI CHAKRASAMVARA VAJRAYOGINI BHYA

The sadhana of glorious Chakrasamvara five deity entitled, *The Lamp Illuminating the Condensed Essence of Great Bliss*.

To Heruka Father and Mother who embrace like a heap of sapphire clouds, I respectfully bow and will compose this method of accomplishment, *A Lamp Illuminating Great Bliss*.

Here for those wishing to practice the sadhana of the bhagawan Heruka Chakrasamvara five deity, assemble the articles of yoga for this ritual.

Then:

Request to the Lineage Gurus

Glorious Heruka, Yogini,
Ghantapa, Rubelshab, Dzalandaripa, Nagpopa,
Guhyapa, Namgyal, Tilopa, Naropa, and to the
Pamtingpa brothers, I make request.

Sherab Tseg, Ma lo, Sachen, Jetsun and his brother,
Sapan, Phakpa, Shangton, Dragpukpa,

Lama Dampa, Jetsun Losang Drak,
And to Khedrup and his brother, I make request.

Dharmavajra, Ensapa father and son,
Chogyen, Kongyen, Tenzin Trinley Shab,
Khetsun, Jamgon, Yongzin, Pandita, and
To Losang Tenzin, I make request.

The lord of secrets manifesting as
A glorious, saffron-robed monk,
All-knowing Dharmabhadra and
His heart-son, the treasure of supreme knowledge,
To my root guru, I make request.

To Ngawang Losang, who perfectly comprehended
The lotus garden of the Conqueror's teachings
And spread unmistaken moral discipline throughout the land
Like a thousand blazing lights,
To the completely qualified guru, I make requests.

With supreme intelligence like the second Buddha,
Accomplishing explanations that blaze like a thousand lamps,
By conjoining the essence of the teachings of sutra and tantra,
To the incomparable glorious guru, I make requests.

You who bear the name of the omniscient Dharmabhadra
And the all-seeing Manjugosha,
To the feet of the kind guru
Namkha Tenkyong Tenzin Tsöndru, I make request.

To Pabongkha—the actual Vajradhara,
And the tutor, the "Incomparable Supreme Son,"
Losang Yeshe Tenzin Gyatso,
I request you, please bless my mental continuum.

May I receive your blessings to manifest the four bodies by
Training my mind through the common path

And upholding commitments of the empowerment,
For the sake of perfecting my practice of the outer and inner gross and
    subtle generation stage
And the five stages of the completion stage.

Going for Refuge and Generating Bodhichitta

Recite three times:

I will always go for refuge
To Buddha, Dharma, and Sangha,
To all three spiritual vehicles,
The dakinis of secret mantra yoga,
The heroes, heroines, and empowering goddesses,
And the bodhisattvas; but especially,
I will always go for refuge to my spiritual master.

To accomplish the welfare of all living beings,
May I become Heruka,
And then lead every living being
To Heruka's supreme state.

In an instant I arise as Heruka together with the Mother.

Blessing the Vajra and Bell

The vajra is method and the bell is wisdom; both together are the nature
of ultimate bodhichitta.

*Hold this thought firmly; now hold the vajra at your heart between the thumb and
the ring finger of your right hand and recite:*

OM SARWA TATHAGATA SIDDHI VAJRA SAMAYA TIKTA EKA
TON DHARAYAMI VAJRA SATTÖ HI HI HI HI HI HUM HUM HUM
PHAT SÖHA

Now hold the bell between the thumb and ring finger of your left hand, and hold it at your left hip while reciting,

OM VAJRA GHANTA HUM

I delight Vajrasattva and the others.

Hold up the vajra while contemplating:

HUM

Brandishing the vajra
Liberates all living beings from confusion.
Joyfully I hold the vajra and
Engage in the Dharma activity of liberation.

HUM HUM HUM HO HO HO

Hold the vajra at your right hip, and play the bell by moving the clapper from the center through the eight directions while reciting,

OM VAJRA DHARMA RANITA, PARANITA, SAMPARANITA, SARWA BUDDHA KHYETRA PATZALINI PENJA PARAMITA NADA SÖBHAWA VAJRA SATTÖ HRIDAYA, SANTO KHANI HUM HUM HUM HO HO HO SÖHA

Blessing the Inner Offering

HA HO HRIH (3x)

In the center of the basis of accomplishment is a red HA, whose light [purifies] color. Below this is a white HO whose light [purifies] scent. Between these is a blue HRIH, whose light [purifies] faults and potential, thus transforming it into nectar.

OM AH HUM (3x)

To the right of the HRIH is a white OM, to the left is a red AH, in front is a blue HUM; by the light rays of these three letters, it is blessed, increases, and becomes vast.

If done briefly:

HA HO HRIH

All faults of color, scent, and potential are purified, and it becomes a great ocean of uncontaminated nectar of exalted wisdom.

OM AH HUM (3x)

Blessing the Outer Offerings

OM KHANDAROHI HUM HUM PHAT
OM SÖBHAWA SHUDDHA SARWA DHARMA SÖBHAWA
SHUDDHO HAM

Everything becomes emptiness.

From the sphere of emptiness, from KAMs, come vast and expansive skull cups, inside of which, from HUMs, come water for drinking, water for bathing, flowers, incense, lights, perfume, food, and music. Their nature is bliss and emptiness in the aspect of the individual offering substances that operate as objects of enjoyment of the six senses to bestow exalted, uncontaminated bliss.

OM AHRGHAM AH HUM
OM PADÄM AH HUM
OM VAJRA PUPE AH HUM
OM VAJRA DHUPE AH HUM
OM VAJRA DIWE AH HUM
OM VAJRA GÄNDHE AH HUM
OM VAJRA NEWIDE AH HUM
OM VAJRA SHAPTA AH HUH

Blessing the Preliminary Torma

HA HO HRIH (3x)

In the center of the basis of accomplishment is a red HA, whose light [purifies] color. Below this is a white HO, whose light [purifies] scent. Between these is a blue HRIH, whose light [purifies] faults and potential, thus transforming it into nectar.

OM AH HUM (3x)

To the right of the HRIH is a white OM, to the left is a red AH, in front is a blue HUM; by the light rays of these three letters, it is blessed and becomes vast.

If done briefly:

HA HO HRIH

All faults of color, scent, and potential are purified, and it becomes a great ocean of uncontaminated nectar of exalted wisdom.

OM AH HUM (3x)

Inviting the Guests of the Preliminary Torma— the Mundane Dakas and Dakinis

PHAIM

From the HUM at my heart, light rays radiate to the places of the directional protectors, field protectors, nagas, and so forth, who abide in the eight charnel grounds, invoking them to the space before me. Those in the eight cardinal and intermediate directions instantly enter into the clear light and arise in the aspect of Heruka Father and Mother. From a HUM at their tongue arises a three-pronged vajra, and through tubes of light the size of only a grain of barley, they partake of the essence of the torma.

Offering the Torma

OM KHA KHA, KHAHI KHAHI, SARWA YAKYA RAKYASA,
BHUTA, PRETA, PISHATSA, UNATA, APAMARA, VAJRA
DAKA, DAKI NÄDAYA, IMAM BALING GRIHANTU, SAMAYA
RAKYANTU, MAMA SARWA SIDDHI METRA YATZANTU,
YATIPAM, YATETAM, BHUDZATA, PIWATA, DZITRATA MATI
TRAMATA, MAMA SARWA KATAYA, SÄDSUKHAM BISHUDAYE,
SAHAYEKA BHAWÄNTU, HUM HUM PHAT PHAT SÖHA (2x)

*With the first recitation, offer the torma to the guests in the cardinal directions,
and with the second, to the guests in the intermediate directions.*

Outer Offerings

OM AHRGHAM PRATITZA SÖHA
OM PADÄM PRATITZA SÖHA
OM VAJRA PUPE PRATITZA SÖHA
OM VAJRA DHUPE PRATITZA SÖHA
OM VAJRA DIWE PRATITZA SÖHA
OM VAJRA GÄNDHE PRATITZA SÖHA
OM VAJRA NEWIDE PRATITZA SÖHA
OM VAJRA SHAPTA PRATITZA SÖHA

Inner Offering

To the mouths of the directional guardians, regional guardians, nagas,
and so forth:

OM AH HUM

Requests

For the sake of protecting the teachings
And accomplishing the welfare of sentient beings,
You have taken oaths and heart commitments.

Great and glorious agents, swift as the mind,
With terrifying bodies and inexhaustible wrath,
Who subdue the vicious and destroy those on the dark side,
Who bestow results to the practice of yoga,
With inconceivable strength, power, and blessing,
To the eight harm-givers and so forth I prostrate.
I request your wives, children, and servants
To bestow the kindness of all attainments.

This is requesting assistance. Then recite the hundred-syllable mantra as a request for forbearance.

OM VAJRA MU

The mundane beings return to their own places.

Blessing the Outer Offerings for the Self-Generation

OM KHANDAROHI HUM HUM PHAT
OM SÖBHAWA SHUDDHA SARWA DHARMA SÖBHAWA
SHUDDHO HAM

Everything becomes emptiness.

From the sphere of emptiness, from KAMs, come vast and expansive skull cups, inside of which, from HUMs, come water for drinking, water for bathing, water for the mouth, flowers, incense, lights, perfume, food, and music. Their nature is bliss and emptiness in the aspect of the individual offering substances that operate as objects of enjoyment of the six senses to bestow exalted, uncontaminated bliss.

OM AHRGHAM AH HUM
OM PADÄM AH HUM
OM ÄNTZAMANAM AH HUM
OM VAJRA PUPE AH HUM
OM VAJRA DHUPE AH HUM

OM VAJRA DIWE AH HUM
OM VAJRA GÄNDHE AH HUM
OM VAJRA NEWIDE AH HUM
OM VAJRA SHAPTA AH HUH

Offer a mandala.

Vajrasattva Meditation and Recitation

On the crown of my head, from a letter PAM, comes a lotus, and from AH, a moon mandala, upon which from HUM, comes a white five-pronged vajra, marked by a HUM. From this, light rays radiate and perform the two purposes.

The light rays return, and this transforms into Vajrasattva, with one face and two hands holding a vajra and bell, sitting in the vajra posture, and embracing his consort Vajra Bhagawati, who has one face and two hands holding a curved knife and skull cup. Both beings are adorned with silks and other various precious ornaments. At both of their crowns is a white OM, at their throats a red AH, and at their hearts a blue HUM.

From the HUM at their hearts light rays radiate and invite the wisdom beings, in the same aspect, to the space before them.

DZA, HUM, BAM, HO

They become nondual.

Again, light rays radiate from the letter HUM at their hearts and invite the empowering deities to the space before them.

"O all you tathagatas, I request you to bestow empowerment upon them."

By requesting in this way, they hold aloft vases filled with the nectar of exalted wisdom and bestow the empowerment.

"OM SARWA TATHAGATA ABHISHEKATA SAMAYA SHRIYE HUM"

Saying this, they grant the empowerment, their whole bodies are filled, and the excess water that overflows on the crown of their heads completely transforms into Akshobya, who becomes their crown ornament.

On a moon disk at his heart is a syllable HUM, surrounded by the hundred-syllable mantra.

O Blessed One Vajrasattva, please cleanse and pacify all the nonvirtues, negative karma, and degenerated commitments of myself and all living beings.

Having been requested in this way, light rays radiate from the letter HUM and the mantra rosary at his heart. This purifies all the negative karma and obscurations of all living beings and makes pleasing offerings to the buddhas and their sons. All the good qualities of their body, speech, and mind are collected in the form of light rays, which dissolve into the HUM and the mantra rosary. From these a stream of white nectar descends from the joined organs of the Father and Mother, the nectar of exalted wisdom enters through the crown of my head, filling my whole body and purifying all the negative karma and obscurations of my three doors.

OM VAJRA HERUKA SAMAYA MANU PALAYA, HERUKA TENO PATITA, DRIDHO ME BHAWA, SUTO KAYO ME BHAWA, SUPO KAYO ME BHAWA, ANURAKTO ME BHAWA, SARWA SIDDHI ME PRAYATZA, SARWA KARMA SUTZA ME, TZITAM SHRIYAM KURU HUM, HA HA HA HA HO BAGAWÄN, VAJRA HERUKA, MA ME MUNTSA, HERUKA BHAWA, MAHA SAMAYA SATTÖ AH HUM PHAT

Recite at least twenty-one times.

Through my ignorance and delusions I have broken or allowed my spiritual commitments to degenerate. O spiritual master, be my refuge and protector. Principal Holder of the Vajra, endowed with great compassion, lord of all living beings, to you I go for refuge.

Then Vajrasattva says:

"Son of the lineage, now your negative karma, obscurations, broken and degenerated commitments are cleansed and purified."

Saying this, he dissolves into me, and my three doors become inseparable from the body, speech, and mind of Vajrasattva.

Inviting the Field of Merit

From the HUM at the heart of myself appearing clearly as Heruka, light rays radiate, invoking my guru who is inseparable from the bhagawan Chakrasamvara and the assembly of deities from Akanishta to the space before me. The light rays then dissolve back into my heart.

Prostration

NAMO GURU CHAKRASAMVARA SARWA DAKINI BHYA

Outer Offering

OM SARWA TATHAGATA AHRGHAM PRATITZA SÖHA
OM SARWA TATHAGATA PADÄM PRATITZA SÖHA
OM SARWA TATHAGATA PUPE PRATITZA SÖHA
OM SARWA TATHAGATA DHUPE PRATITZA SÖHA
OM SARWA TATHAGATA DIWE PRATITZA SÖHA
OM SARWA TATHAGATA GÄNDHE PRATITZA SÖHA
OM SARWA TATHAGATA NEWIDE PRATITZA SÖHA
OM SARWA TATHAGATA SHAPTA PRATITZA SÖHA

Inner Offering

OM SARWA TATHAGATA, OM AH HUM

Secret and Suchness Offering

Father and Mother enter into embrace and experience the exalted wisdom of bliss and emptiness. This is the secret and suchness offerings.

Offering Our Practice and Taking Bodhisattva Vows

Recite three times:

I go for refuge to the Three Jewels
And confess each of my negative actions;
I rejoice in the virtues of migrating beings
And hold with my mind a buddha's enlightenment.

Bringing Death into the Path of the Truth Body

The field of merit dissolves into me, and I receive their blessings.

OM SHUNYATA GYANA VARJA SÖBHAWA ÄMAKO HAM

All phenomena, all worlds and beings dissolve into me, and I too dissolve into unobservable emptiness.

Bringing the Intermediate State into the Path of the Enjoyment Body

From the state of emptiness where all appearances have gathered like this, my mind appears in the form of a nada standing upright in space, white with a shade of red.

Setting up the Protection Circle and Bringing Rebirth into the Path of the Emanation Body

Instantly, from the state of emptiness, comes a vajra ground, tent, canopy, web of arrows, and fire. In the center of this are the four elements, stacked one above the other. Upon this are Mount Meru and a variegated lotus, in the center of which is a variegated double vajra. Upon this is an eight- petaled variegated lotus, in the center of which are the vowels and consonants whose nature are the marks and signs [of an enlightened being]. These two completely transform into a moon mandala, white with a shade of red. The mirrorlike appearance of the vowels, consonants, and moon represents the exalted mirrorlike wisdom and the exalted wisdom of equality.

I, the nada, standing in space, see below me the moon, white with a shade of red, the nature of the red and white bodhichittas of Buddha Father and Mother, and with the strong intention to fulfill the welfare of all living beings, enter into the center of the moon. Gradually, the letter HUM emerges, white with a shade of red, which represents the exalted wisdom of discrimination. From the HUM, light rays radiate and accomplish the two purposes, collect back, and dissolve into the nada, and the letter HUM becomes the nature of spontaneous joy, which represents the exalted wisdom of accomplishing activities.

OM AH HUM
OM SARWA BIRA YOGINI KAYA WAKA CHITTA VAJRA SÖBHAWA
ÄMAKO HAM
OM VAJRA SHUDDHA SARWA DHARMA VAJRA SHUDDHO HAM

The moon, vowels, consonants, and HUM completely transform, and the entire supporting and supported mandalas arise all at once, which represents the exalted wisdom of the dharmadhatu.

Furthermore, the celestial mansion is constructed like a square house with four doorways, ornaments, and archways, complete with all the characteristics. In the very center is a lotus of various colors and a sun seat. Upon this lotus I arise as the bhagawan Heruka with a dark blue body, four faces, and twelve arms. My principal face is dark blue, my left face green, my rear face red, and my right face yellow. Each face has three eyes, with a rosary of five-pronged vajras on each forehead. My right leg is outstretched and suppresses the head of black Bhairava; my bent left leg suppresses the breast of red Kalarati.

My first two hands hold a vajra and bell, and embrace Vajravarahi. The next two hands are outstretched and hold an elephant skin while making threatening mudras. My third right hand holds a damaru, the fourth an axe, the fifth a curved knife, and the sixth a three-pointed spear. My third left hand holds a katvanga, marked with a vajra, the fourth a skull cup filled with blood, the fifth a vajra noose, and the sixth a four-faced head of Brahma. My hair is tied up on the crown of my head and marked with a variegated vajra. Each forehead is adorned with a crown of five skulls. On the left side of my head is a slightly crooked crescent moon. My faces change, and my four sets of four fangs are bared and terrifying. I display nine moods: three physical moods of haughtiness, heroism, and repulsion; three verbal moods of laughter, wrath, and fearfulness; and three mental moods of compassion, wonder, and peace. I wear a lower garment of a tiger's skin and a long necklace of fifty human heads strung together with human intestines. Adorned with the six mudras, my entire body is smeared with the ashes of human bones.

As the bhagawan I am embracing the bhagawati Vajravarahi with a red-colored body, one face, two hands, and three eyes. Her left hand, embracing the Father's neck, holds a skull cup filled with the blood of the four maras and so forth, which is being offered to the Father's mouth. Her right hand threatens vicious beings by holding a curved knife with the threatening mudra. Her three eyes are blazing red like fire. Her two calves are wrapped around the Father's thighs. She is the nature of great compassion. Adorned with five mudras, she wears five human skulls and a necklace of fifty human skulls.

In the eastern direction of the eight petals of the lotus is black Dakini; in the north, green Lama; in the west, red Kandharohi; and in the south, yellow Rupini. They all have one face and four hands; their two right hands hold a curved knife and damaru, the two left hold a skull cup and katvanga. They are naked with loosely hanging hair. Adorned with the five mudras, they wear a crown of five human skulls and a long necklace of fifty human skulls, and stand with their right legs outstretched.

In the intermediate directions are four vases filled with nectar, upon which are four skull cups filled with bodhichitta.

Blessing the Four Chakras

At the Father's navel and heart and the Mother's throat and forehead are moon cushions, with the Mother's essence and near-essence mantras.

At the Mother's navel and heart and the Father's throat and forehead are sun cushions, with the Father's essence and near-essence mantras.

The mantras are red in color, and light rays radiate back and forth, touching and embracing each other.

Blessing the Secret Places of the Father and Mother

From the secret place of the Father, from a white HUM, there arises a white five-pronged vajra, and from a red BÄ, there arises a red jewel, marked with a yellow BÄ.

From the secret place of the Mother, from an AH, there arises a red, three-petaled lotus, and from a white DÄ, there arises a white stamen, signifying white bodhichitta, marked with a yellow DÄ.

OM AH HUM

By entering into embrace, I generate the four joys that are drawn out in stages. The inseparability of great bliss and emptiness is actually the thirty-seven aspects of enlightenment, reflected as the five deities who appear like a rainbow in the sky.

Putting on the Armor

At my heart on a moon seat is white OM AH, the nature of Vajrasattva. At my head on a sun seat is yellow NAMA HI, the nature of Vairochana. At my crown on a sun seat is red SÖHA HU, the nature of Pämanarteshvara. At my two shoulders on a sun seat is black BOKE HE, the nature of glorious Heruka. At my two eyes on a sun seat is orange HUM HUM HO, the nature of Vajrasurya. At my forehead on a sun seat is green PHAT HAM, the nature of Paramashawa.

At the Principal Mother's navel on a sun seat is red OM BAM, the nature of Vajravarahi. At her heart on a sun is blue HAM YAM, the nature of Yamani. At her throat on a moon is white HRIM MOM, the nature of Mohani. At her head on a sun is yellow HRIM HRIM, the nature of Sachalani. At her crown on a sun is green HUM HUM, the nature of Samtrasani. At her forehead on a sun seat is smoke-colored PHAT PHAT, the nature of Chandika.

At the crown of each deity, on a moon is a letter OM, at their throats on a lotus is a letter AH, and at their hearts on a sun is a letter HUM.

Invoking the Wisdom Beings

PHAIM

Light rays radiate from the letter HUM at my heart, invoking the wisdom beings identical to the meditation beings, together with empowering and offering goddesses, to the space before me. The light then dissolves back into my heart.

OM KHANDAROHI HUM HUM PHAT

All interfering spirits are dispelled.

OM AHRGHAM PRATITZA AH HUM

DZA, HUM, BAM, HO

We become nondual.

OM YOGA SHUDDHA SARWA DHARMA YOGA SHUDDHO HAM

Bestowing Empowerment

OM AHRGHAM PRATITZA AH HUM

"O all you tathagatas please bestow the empowerment."

Having been requested this way, they bestow the empowerment, saying,

"OM SARWA TATHAGATA ABHISHEKATA SAMAYA SHRIYE HUM"

Saying this, the empowering deities grant the empowerment. The Principal is adorned by Vajrasattva Vajravarahi by Akshobya and the four dakinis by Ratnasambhava. The empowering deities dissolve into me.

Bless the offerings.

Offerings to the Self-Generation

OM SARWA TATHAGATA AHRGHAM PRATITZA SÖHA
OM SARWA TATHAGATA PADÄM PRATITZA SÖHA
OM SARWA TATHAGATA ÄNTZAMANAM PRATITZA SÖHA
OM SARWA TATHAGATA PUPE PRATITZA SÖHA
OM SARWA TATHAGATA DHUPE PRATITZA SÖHA
OM SARWA TATHAGATA DIWE PRATITZA SÖHA
OM SARWA TATHAGATA GÄNDHE PRATITZA SÖHA
OM SARWA TATHAGATA NEWIDE PRATITZA SÖHA
OM SARWA TATHAGATA SHAPTA PRATITZA SÖHA

Inner Offering

To the mouth of my kind root and lineage gurus, the glorious and holy gurus, I offer, OM AH HUM

OM HRIH HA HA HUM HUM PHAT, OM AH HUM

OM SARWA BUDDHA DAKINIYE VAJRA WARNARNIYE HUM HUM PHAT SÖHA, OM AH HUM

OM DAKINIYE HUM HUM PHAT, OM AH HUM
OM LAME HUM HUM PHAT, OM AH HUM
OM KHANDAROHI HUM HUM PHAT, OM AH HUM
OM RUPINIYE HUM HUM PHAT, OM AH HUM

To the collection of yidams and mandala deities, OM AH HUM

To the powerful guardians and protectors of the Dharma, OM AH HUM

To the heroes, yoginis, directional protectors, regional protectors, nagas, and so forth, OM AH HUM

To all the guardians of the local places and to all sentient beings transformed to the deity, OM AH HUM

Secret and Suchness Offering

The Father and Mother enter into embrace and generate the four joys of the simultaneous born bliss and emptiness, and are delighted by the offering of thatness.

Offering Praise with the Mantras

OM SHRI VAJRA HE HE RU RU KAM HUM HUM PHAT DAKINI
DZALA SHAMBARAM SÖHA

OM VAJRA BEROTZANIYE HUM HUM PHAT SÖHA

OM DAKINIYE HUM HUM PHAT
OM LAME HUM HUM PHAT
OM KHANDAROHI HUM HUM PHAT
OM RUPINIYE HUM HUM PHAT

Eight Lines of Praise to Heruka Father and Mother

OM NAMO BHAGAWATE WIRE SHAYA HUM HUM PHAT
OM MAHA KÄLWA AHGNI SAMNI BHAYA HUM HUM PHAT
OM DZATA MUGUTRA KORTAYA HUM HUM PHAT
OM DHAMKHATRA KARA LOTRA BHIKHANA MUKAYA
    HUM HUM PHAT
OM SAHARA BHUNDZA BHASURAYA HUM HUM PHAT
OM PARASHUWA SHODHÄDA SHULA KHATAMGA DHARINE
    HUM HUM PHAT
OM BHÄGADZINAM WARA DHARAYA HUM HUM PHAT
OM MAHA DHUMA ÄNDHAKARA WAWUKAYA HUM HUM
    PHAT

OM NAMO BHAGAWATI VAJRA VARAHI BAM HUM HUM PHAT

OM NAMO ARYA APARADZITE TRE LOKYA MATI BIYE SHÖRI
HUM HUM PHAT
OM NAMA SARWA BUTA BHAYA WAHI MAHA VAJRE HUM HUM
PHAT
OM NAMO VAJRA SANI ADZITE APARADZITE WASHAM
KARANITRA HUM HUM PHAT
OM NAMO BHRAMANI SHOKANI ROKANI KROTE KARALENI
HUM HUM PHAT
OM NAMA DRASANI MARANI PRABHE DANI PARADZAYE HUM
HUM PHAT
OM NAMO BIDZAYE DZAMBHANI TAMBHANI MOHANI HUM
HUM PHAT
OM NAMO VAJRA VARAHI MAHA YOGINI KAME SHÖRI KHAGE
HUM HUM PHAT

Offering of Praise

O Great and Glorious Hero Heruka
Having control over your pure vajra,
To Vajravarahi and those
Powerful heroes and heroines
In the places, near places, fields,
Meeting places, and charnel grounds,
Who generate great attachment in the minds of your devotees,
To all of you respectfully I prostrate.

During the meditation session you should principally focus on the generation stage, then when you are tired say the mantras. At this point make an effort to meditate single-pointedly upon the profound yoga of the generation stage.

Mantra Recitation

The mala transforms into vajra speech.

Having blessed [the rosary], engage in the following visualization during the recitation:

At the heart of myself as the deity, on a sun seat is a letter HUM, surrounded by the mantra rosary arranged counterclockwise. From the HUM in the center mandala, deities radiate out, performing the welfare of migrating beings. Once again light rays radiate out, collect back, and dissolve into the letter HUM.

Recite the essence mantra of the Principal:

OM SHRI VAJRA HE HE RU RU KAM HUM HUM PHAT DAKINI DZALA SHAMBARAM SÖHA

Recite the near-essence mantra:

OM HRIH HA HA HUM HUM PHAT

Recite the essence mantra of the Mother:

OM VAJRA BEROTZANIYE HUM HUM PHAT SÖHA

Recite the near-essence mantra:

OM SARWA BUDDHA DAKINIYE VAJRA WARNANIYE HUM HUM PHAT SÖHA

Recite the mantras of the four heart dakinis:

OM DAKINIYE HUM HUM PHAT

OM LAME HUM HUM PHAT
OM KHANDAROHI HUM HUM PHAT
OM RUPINIYE HUM HUM PHAT

Recite the hundred-syllable mantra.

During an approximation retreat it is necessary to offer tormas every day. During your sessions if you want to offer a torma do it as follows.

Torma Offering

Blessing the Torma

Now bless the torma in the same way as the inner offering.

Invoking the Guests of the Torma Offering

PHAIM

From the letter HUM at my heart, light rays radiate and invoke the directional protectors, field protectors, nagas, and so forth, who abide in the eight charnel grounds, together with the mandala of Heruka, to the space before me.

Offering the Torma

From a HUM at their tongue arises a three-pronged vajra, and through tubes of light the size of only a grain of barley they partake of the essence of the torma.

OM VAJRA AH RA LI HO: DZA HUM BAM HO: VAJRA DAKINI SAMAYA TÖN TRISHAYA HO (3x)

With the first recitation, offer the torma to the Principal Father; with the second to the Principal Mother; and with the third to the four dakinis, beginning in the east and offering counterclockwise.

Outer Offerings

OM SARWA TATHAGATA AHRGHAM PRATITZA SÖHA
OM SARWA TATHAGATA PADÄM PRATITZA SÖHA
OM SARWA TATHAGATA PUPE PRATITZA SÖHA
OM SARWA TATHAGATA DHUPE PRATITZA SÖHA
OM SARWA TATHAGATA DIWE PRATITZA SÖHA
OM SARWA TATHAGATA GÄNDHE PRATITZA SÖHA

OM SARWA TATHAGATA NEWIDE PRATITZA SÖHA
OM SARWA TATHAGATA SHAPTA PRATITZA SÖHA

Inner Offering

OM HRIH HA HA HUM HUM PHAT, OM AH HUM

OM SARWA BUDDHA DAKINIYE VAJRA WARNARNIYE HUM
HUM PHAT SÖHA, OM AH HUM

OM DAKINIYE HUM HUM PHAT, OM AH HUM

OM LAME HUM HUM PHAT, OM AH HUM

OM KHANDAROHI HUM HUM PHAT, OM AH HUM

OM RUPINIYE HUM HUM PHAT, OM AH HUM

Eight Lines of Praise to the Father

OM I prostrate to the bhagawan, powerful lord of the heroes HUM
HUM PHAT

OM To you with a light equal to the fire of the great eon HUM HUM
PHAT

OM To you who possess an inexhaustible crown of hair HUM HUM
PHAT

OM To you with a terrifying face and bared fangs HUM HUM PHAT

OM To you who have a thousand arms of blazing light HUM HUM
PHAT

OM To you who hold an axe, a noose, a spear, and a katvanga HUM
HUM PHAT

OM To you who wear a tiger-skin garment HUM HUM PHAT

OM I bow to you whose great, smoke-colored body destroys all
obstructions HUM HUM PHAT

Eight Lines of Praise to the Mother

OM I prostrate to the bhagawati Vajravarahi HUM HUM PHAT

OM To the powerful Arya Knowledge-Goddess, invincible in the three realms HUM HUM PHAT

OM To you who destroy with your great vajra the fear of all demons HUM HUM PHAT

OM To you whose eyes empower those who sit on the vajra seat not to be overcome by others HUM HUM PHAT

OM To you whose wrathful body of psychic heat can desiccate Brahma HUM HUM PHAT

OM To you who terrify and dry up demons and thus can vanquish other forces HUM HUM PHAT

OM To you who conquer all that makes us dull, excited, and confused HUM HUM PHAT

OM I bow to the consort Vajravarahi, the dakini who has the power of desire HUM HUM PHAT

Requesting the Fulfillment of Wishes

You who have destroyed equally the conceptions attached to samsara and peace,
And are endowed with the spacelike vision of all things,
O Protector, by the moisture of your great compassion and strong love,
May the goddesses truly take me under their loving care.

Offering the Torma to the Mundane Dakas and Dakinis

The directional protectors, field protectors, nagas, and so forth, who abide in the eight charnel grounds instantly enter into the clear light and arise in the aspect of Heruka Father and Mother. From a HUM at their tongues arises a three-pronged vajra, and through tubes of light the size of only a grain of barley, they partake of the essence of the torma.

OM KHA KHA, KHAHI KHAHI, SARWA YAKYA RAKYASA, BHUTA, PRETA, PISHATSA, UNATA, APAMARA, VAJRA

DAKA, DAKI NÄDAYA, IMAM BALING GRIHANTU, SAMAYA
RAKYANTU, MAMA SARWA SIDDHI METRAYATZANTU,
YATIPAM, YATETAM, BHUDZATA, PIWATA, DZITRATA MATI
TRAMATA, MAMA SARWA KATAYA, SÄDSUKHAM BISHUDAYE,
SAHAYEKA BHAWÄNTU, HUM HUM PHAT PHAT SÖHA (2X)

Outer Offerings

OM AHRGHAM PRATITZA SÖHA
OM PADÄM PRATITZA SÖHA
OM VAJRA PUPE AH HUM SÖHA
OM VAJRA DHUPE AH HUM SÖHA
OM VAJRA DIWE AH HUM SÖHA
OM VAJRA GÄNDHE AH HUM SÖHA
OM VAJRA NEWIDE AH HUM SÖHA
OM VAJRA SHAPTA AH HUM SÖHA

Inner Offering

To the mouths of the directional guardians, regional guardians, nagas, and
so forth, OM AH HUM.

Requests

For the sake of protecting the teachings
And accomplishing the welfare of sentient beings,
You have taken oaths and heart commitments.
Great and glorious agents, swift as the mind,
With terrifying bodies and inexhaustible wrath,
Who subdue the vicious and destroy those on the dark side,
Who bestow results to the practice of yoga,
With inconceivable strength, power, and blessing,
To the eight harm-givers and so forth, I prostrate.
I request your wives, children, and servants
To bestow the kindness of all attainments.

OM VAJRA MU

The mundane beings return to their own places.

OM YOGA SHUDDHA SARWA DHARMA YOGA SHUDDHO
   HAM

The deities and mandala in front dissolve into me.

If you want to make the torma offering shorter, do the first part the same as above up to the inner offering to the deity, then:

OM SARWA TATHAGATA, OM AH HUM

Respectfully I prostrate to the lotus feet of
The supreme guru-deity Heruka,
The always-loving, venerable Mother,
And to the powerful heroes and heroines.

Then make request for your wishes:

To the collection of mandala deities, please pacify unfavorable circumstances, obstacles, and hindrances in all directions of myself and all living beings, and please bestow your blessing to accomplish all our wishes and collect all excellent favorable conditions.

Then request actions from the worldly beings:

Directional protectors, regional protectors, nagas, and so forth,
Please accept this cloud of torma offerings,
And may I, the yogi, and my retinue
Receive all the attainments we desire.

Then:

From the HUM at my heart, light rays radiate, the supporting mandala dissolves into the retinue; the retinue dissolves into the four faces; I, Father and Mother, dissolve into the letter HUM; the HUM completely transforms; and I appear clearly as Heruka with my three places marked by OM AH HUM.

Dedication

Glorious Heruka, your body with disciplined attachment blazes
    throughout the three realms,
With thousands of blue light rays as brilliant as a hundred thousand suns;
May I dance simultaneously with the
Many passionate beings of your body.

By the truth of the valid goddesses, with valid commitments,
And the supreme valid explanations they have taught,
May the goddesses
Take us into their care.

To accomplish the welfare of all living beings
May I become Heruka,
And then lead every living being
To Heruka's supreme state.

In that way make the dedication prayers. When completing the generation stage, say the auspicious verses that begin: "The day of bliss and excellence . . ." Between sessions, abandon the ordinary appearance and conception of your three doors, and while abiding in the Brahmin conduct, engage in the yogas of sleeping, rising, washing, eating, and so forth, and make your life of leisure meaningful.

The ocean of secret precepts of Guru Manjushri,
Upheld by Losang Chökyi Gyaltsen,
Was churned with the spoon of incomparable wisdom,
And produced the butter of this stainless excellent explanation,
The essence of which has been examined in detail by those with
    precise intellect.

To illuminate this yoga method, I have composed this precious vessel of blazing verses entitled *A Lamp Illuminating the Supreme Path of Great Bliss*.

May we have the good fortune to encounter your body and speech, which
Blaze brightly with the exalted wisdom of great bliss
And completely dispel the darkness conceiving true existence in the
The minds of migrating beings.

This concludes the sadhana of the glorious Heruka Chakrasamvara five deity entitled, *A Lamp Illuminating the Condensed Essence of Great Bliss*. This sadhana was compiled from Panchen Losang Chökyi Gyaltsen's sadhana, entitled *Source of Great Bliss*. These days, the intellect and diligence of living beings are very weak, as is their wish to practice; also our minds are equally obscured. Thus it is difficult to understand the order of the ritual. So, for the sake of helping those beings, with superior intention, I, the noble Yangchen Drupay Dorje, have drawn from the intention and view of the all-knowing Dharmabhadra Palsangpo and composed this text on the first day of Saka Dawa at the peak of Ganden Mountain at Ngulchu, in the Vajra Palace Cave, and it was scribed by Zong Chö Losang Tenzin.

May Virtue Increase
SARVA MANGALAM

Panchen Lama Losang Chökyi Gyaltsen's
Guru Yoga for the Five Stages of Completion of Ghantapa

Going for Refuge and Generating Bodhichitta

At all times I go for refuge
To Buddha, Dharma, and Sangha,
In all three vehicles,
The dakinis of secret mantra yoga,
The heroes, heroines, and powerful goddess,
In the great beings, the bodhisattvas;
But above all others, at all times
I take refuge in my spiritual master.

For the welfare of all living beings
May I become Heruka,
And then lead every living being
To Heruka's supreme state. (3x)

Four Immeasurables

May all beings come to possess the special bliss of the aryas.
May all beings be freed from suffering and the causes of suffering.
May all beings never be separated from the bliss they have obtained.
May all beings be free from delusions and the secondary delusions.

Self-Generation

From the letter HUM at my heart, light rays radiate and melt all worlds and their beings into light, which dissolve into me, and I too melt into light and dissolve into the clear light. I am the truth body of Heruka.

From the sphere of emptiness, my mind appears as a shaft of blue light. I am the enjoyment body of Heruka.

This completely transforms, and I arise as Heruka with one face and two hands, holding a vajra and bell and embracing the Mother Vajravarahi. I am the emanation body of Heruka.

Vajrasattva Meditation and Recitation

On the crown of my head, from PAM, comes a lotus, and from AH, a moon mandala, upon which, from HUM, comes a white, five-pronged vajra marked by a HUM. From this, light rays radiate and perform the two purposes. The light rays return, and this transforms into Vajrasattva, with one face and two hands, holding a vajra and bell. He sits in the vajra posture and embraces his consort Vajra Bhagawati, who has one face and two hands, holding a curved knife and skull cup. Both beings are adorned with silks and a variety of other precious ornaments.

At both of their crowns is a white OM, at their throats, a red AH, and at their hearts, a blue HUM. From the HUM at their hearts, light rays radiate and invite the wisdom beings, in the same aspect, to the space before them.

DZA HUM BAM HO

They become nondual.

Again, light rays radiate from the letter HUM at their hearts and invite the empowering deities to the space before them.

"O all you tathagatas, I request you to bestow the empowerment upon them."

By requesting in this way, they hold aloft vases filled with the nectar of exalted wisdom and bestow the empowerment.

"OM SARWA TATHAGATA ABHISHEKATA SAMAYA SHRIYE HUM"

Saying this, they grant the empowerment. Their whole bodies are filled, and the excess water that overflows from the crown of their heads completely transforms into Akshobya, who becomes their crown ornament.

On a moon disk at his heart is a syllable HUM, surrounded by the hundred-syllable mantra.

O Blessed One, Vajrasattva, please cleanse and pacify all the nonvirtues, negative karma, and degenerated commitments of myself and all living beings.

Having been requested in this way, light rays radiate from the letter HUM and the mantra rosary at his heart. This purifies all the negative karma and obscurations of all living beings and makes pleasing offerings to the buddhas and their sons. All the good qualities of their body, speech, and mind are collected in the form of light rays, which dissolve into the HUM and the mantra rosary. From these a stream of white nectar descends from the joined organs of the Father and Mother, and the nectar of exalted wisdom enters through the crown of my head, filling my whole body and purifying all the negative karma and obscurations of my three doors.

OM VAJRA HERUKA SAMAYA MANU PALAYA, HERUKA TENO PATITA, DRIDHO ME BHAWA, SUTO KAYO ME BHAWA, SUPO KAYO ME BHAWA, ANURAKTO ME BHAWA, SARWA SIDDHI ME PRAYATZA, SARWA KARMA SUTZA ME, TZITAM SHRIYAM KURU HUM, HA HA HA HA HO BAGAWÄN, VAJRA HERUKA, MA ME MUNTSA, HERUKA BHAWA, MAHA SAMAYA SATTÖ AH HUM PHAT

[*Recite at least twenty-one times.*]

Through my ignorance and delusions, I have broken and caused my spiritual commitments to degenerate. O spiritual master, be my refuge and protector. Principal Holder of the Vajra, endowed with great compassion, lord of all living beings, to you I go for refuge.

Then Vajrasattva says:

"Son of the lineage, now your negative karma, obscurations, broken and degenerated commitments are cleansed and purified."

Saying this, he dissolves into me, and my three doors become inseparable from the body, speech, and mind of Vajrasattva.

Meditation on Guru Yoga

I arise in the aspect of Heruka Father and Mother with one face and two hands. At the tip of my topknot of hair is an extremely vast, precious jeweled throne upheld by eight snow lions. Upon this is a letter PAM that melts into light and transforms into an eight-petaled lotus of various colors that symbolizes not being polluted by the faults of samsara. In the center of this is the nature of the method of the exalted wisdom of great bliss, in the aspect of a red letter RAM, which melts and arises as a sun mandala. Upon this, symbolizing the exalted wisdom of emptiness, is a white letter AH, which melts and arises as a moon mandala. Upon this, the nature of all the buddhas of the three times, is my root guru in the aspect of all-pervasive conqueror Vajradhara, with a blue-colored body, one face, and two hands. His right hand holds a vajra and his left a bell, and he embraces the Mother Vajradhatu Ishvari, who has a blue-colored body, holds a curved knife and skull cup, and embraces the Father. They both have precious jeweled crown ornaments, ear ornaments, necklaces, bracelets, and anklets, and are adorned with a variety of precious jewels. Their upper bodies are draped in fine silks, and their lower bodies with garments; they are adorned with the thirty-two major marks and eighty minor indications. The Father sits in the vajra position and the Mother in the lotus position. Seeing their bodies dispels all unknowing. I will never be satisfied looking at their bodies. The mere sight of them causes an afterglow of goose bumps. His speech possesses sixty melodies by which he can answer all questions with one voice so that all understand it in their own language. His mind of inconceivable exalted wisdom knows both conventional and ultimate realities. With his great love he views all living beings with compassion as if each were his only child.

Offering Praise

The ornament wheels of your body, speech, and mind are inexhaustible secrets. Your five aggregates are the five [buddha] families. Your four elements are the four Mothers. Your sources, joints, and so forth, are male and female bodhisattvas. Your limbs are the wrathful protectors. Your twenty-one thousand pores are in essence Mahayana arhats, and all of your pores are filled with buddhas and bodhisattvas appearing as a limitless array of buddha lands beyond measure, countless, equaling the atoms in the worldly realms. You reveal inconceivable emanations of your body, speech, and mind, enacting the twelve deeds, purifying all realms, and turning the vast wheel of Dharma according to the fortune of each sentient being, fulfilling the immeasurable needs of migrating beings. In short, your body appears in all realms, and the array of your body, speech, and mind, as well as your enlightened actions, pervades all realms, displaying immeasurable miracles.

At his crown, in the center of the channel wheel, on a moon, is a white OM. At his throat, in the center of the channel wheel, on a lotus, is a red AH. At his heart, in the center of the channel wheel, on a sun, is a blue HUM. From the HUM at his heart limitless light rays radiate to the ten directions and invoke the lineage gurus, peaceful and wrathful deities, a limitless collection of deities, buddhas, and bodhisattvas, surrounded by a collection of heroes, dakinis, and dharma protectors, who dissolve into my root guru in the aspect of Vajradhara.

DZA, HUM, BAM, HO

They become nondual with the commitment beings.

The guru is the embodiment of all gurus,
The embodiment of all deities,
The embodiment of all dharma protectors.
In short, his nature is the embodiment of all
Three [objects] of refuge.

Prostration

By whose kindness the state of great bliss
Can be obtained in an instant,
At the feet of my jewel-like guru,
The vajra holder, I prostrate.

His complete enjoyment body is ablaze with the glory of magnificent signs and indications.

[*Say this expression and make prostrations.*]

Outer Offerings

OM AHRGHAM PRATITZA SÖHA
OM PADÄM PRATITZA SÖHA
OM VAJRA PUPE AH HUM SÖHA
OM VAJRA DHUPE AH HUM SÖHA
OM VAJRA DIWE AH HUM SÖHA
OM VAJRA GÄNDHE AH HUM SÖHA
OM VAJRA NEWIDE AH HUM SÖHA
OM VAJRA SHAPTA AH HUM SÖHA

OM AH VAJRA ADARSHE HUM
OM AH VAJRA WINI HUM
OM AH VAJRA GÄNDHE HUM
OM AH VAJRA RASE HUM
OM AH VAJRA PARSHE HUM
OM AH VAJRA DHARME HUM

Inner Offering

I offer the drink of China tea, endowed with a hundred flavors,
With a perfect sweet scent and the radiance of saffron,
That is the five hooks, the five lamps, and so forth,
And is purified, transformed, and increased into an ocean of nectar.

Secret Offering

I offer beautiful, voluptuous, illusory-like consorts,
A host of messengers born from mantra, from places, and spontaneously
   born,
With slender figures, glowing with youth,
And skilled in the sixty-four arts of love.

Suchness Offerings

I offer you the supreme ultimate bodhichitta
Beyond words, thoughts, and expressions,
The sphere of reality, all phenomena free from the
Elaborations of inherent existence as the great exalted wisdom of
Spontaneous bliss liberated from obstruction.

The Remaining Limbs of Confessing, Rejoicing, Requesting, Beseeching, and Dedication

With fierce regret I confess all nonvirtues and promise to refrain from
   them in the future.
I rejoice in all of the virtues of all beings, both myself and others.
I request the buddhas to turn the wheel of the vast and profound
   Dharma.
Please do not pass into nirvana but remain in the world as long as
   sentient beings exist.
I dedicate all of my virtues to great enlightenment.

The Seven Complete Purities

I go for refuge to the Three Jewels
And confess each of my negative actions.
I rejoice in the virtues of migrating beings
And hold with my mind a buddha's enlightenment.

To Buddha, Dharma, and the Supreme Assembly
I go for refuge until I am enlightened,
And to accomplish the welfare of myself and others
I will generate the mind of enlightenment.

Having generated the mind of supreme enlightenment,
I shall invite all living beings to be my guest,
To engage in the pleasing, supreme practices of enlightenment.
May I attain buddhahood to benefit living beings.

[If you wish to make a long mandala offering, extract it from another source; otherwise, make the short mandala offering as presented below.]

Mandala Offering

The ground sprinkled with perfume and strewn with flowers,
The great mountain, four continents, sun and moon,
Perceived as a buddha land and offered as such—
May all beings enjoy such pure lands.

IDAM GURU RATNA MANDALA KHAM NIRYA TAYA MI

[With stable visualization, emanate with your mind a great land, and then make the following request:]

I request you, my precious guru, whose nature is the embodiment
of all buddhas;
I request you, my precious guru, whose nature is the embodiment
of all holy Dharma;

I request you, my precious guru, whose nature is the embodiment
   of all Sangha;
I request you, my precious guru, whose nature is the embodiment
   of all yidams;
I request you, my precious guru, whose nature is the embodiment
   of all Three [Jewels of] refuge.
Please grant your blessing that my mind moves toward the Dharma.
Please grant your blessing that I may move toward the path of Dharma.
Please grant your blessing that obstacles to the Dharma will not arise.
Please grant your blessing that I may stop all wrong views, from lack
   of faith in the virtuous friend up to the two types of self-grasping.
Please grant your blessing that I may generate all the realizations in my
   mental continuum, from proper reliance upon the virtuous friend to
   death and impermanence, cause and effect of karma, renunciation,
   bodhichitta, the exalted wisdom realizing selflessness, and so forth,
   and may I never generate wrong views.
Please grant your blessing that I may generate the direct realization
   of the profound two stages of the path.

[*Make this request from the depth of your heart.*]

From the OM at the crown of the guru, limitless white light rays and nectar arise and enter through the crown of my head. My whole body is filled, and all the sickness, harm from spirits, negative karma, and obscurations and their imprints that I have accumulated with my body since beginningless lives are cleansed and purified. I receive the vase empowerment and receive the potential to attain the vajra body and the emanation body.

From the AH at the throat of the guru, limitless red light rays and nectar arise and enter through my throat. My whole body is filled, and all the sickness, harm from spirits, negative karma, and obscurations and their imprints that I have accumulated with my speech since beginningless lives are cleansed and purified. I receive the secret empowerment and receive the potential to attain the vajra speech and the enjoyment body.

From the HUM at the heart of the guru, limitless blue light rays and nectar arise and enter through my heart. My whole body is filled and all the sickness, harm from spirits, negative karma, and obscurations and their imprints that I have accumulated with my mind since beginningless lives are cleansed and purified. I receive the exalted-wisdom empowerment and receive the potential to attain the vajra mind and the truth body.

Once again, from the three seed syllables at the three places of the guru, limitless white, red, and blue light rays and nectars arise and enter through the crown of my head, throat, and heart. My whole body is filled, and all the sickness, harm from spirits, negative karma, and obscurations and their imprints that I have accumulated with my body, speech, and mind since beginningless lives are cleansed and purified. I receive the fourth empowerment, and my body, speech, and mind become inseparable from the three secrets, and I attain the good fortune to be able to attain the state of union of Vajradhara.

[*Then, make the request:*]

My glorious and precious root guru, please sit on the lotus and moon
    seat at my heart;
Please care for me through your great kindness,
And grant me the blessings of your body, speech, and mind.

Due to this my guru is delighted and comes to sit on the crown of my head, whereby he melts into bodhichitta, descends through my central channel, and dissolves into the indestructible drop at my heart. My body, speech, and mind become inseparable from the body, speech, and mind of my guru.

[*Imagine:*]

My very subtle wind and mind become the nature of the body, speech, and mind of my guru.

[*At this point meditate on the five stages of completion stage of Mahasiddha Ghantapa as explained in the commentary.*]

Dedication

By this virtue may I quickly
Attain the state of glorious Guru,
Then lead each living being
Without exception to that state.

[*Or make extensive prayers such as*:]

Glorious Heruka, your body with disciplined attachment blazes
    throughout
The three realms with a thousand blue light rays as brilliant as a
    hundred thousand suns.
May the many passionate beings of your bodily
Parts all simultaneously dance.

By the truth of the valid goddesses,
Their valid commitments,
And the supremely valid words they have spoken,
May my virtues be the cause for me to be cared for by the goddesses.

For the sake of all living beings,
May I become Heruka,
And then lead every living being
To Heruka's supreme state.

[*If you wish to make extensive prayers, see the Heruka body mandala sadhana of Pabongkha Rinpoche, entitled "Increasing the Realization of Great Bliss," which contains the dedication prayer of the five stages composed by Lama Tsongkhapa.*]

Heruka Five Deity Tsok Offering Sadhana

OM SVATI

Here is the tsok offering for Heruka Chakrasamvara five deity:

Arrange the meat, alcohol, torma, and so forth, and bless it like the inner offering.

Blessing the Tsok Offering

HA HO HRIH (3x)

In the center of the inner offering container is a red HA, [purifying] color. Below this is a white HO, [purifying] scent. Between these is a blue HRIH, [purifying] faults and potential, thus transforming it into nectar.

OM AH HUM (3x)

To the right of the HRIH is a white OM, to the left is a red AH, and in front is a blue HUM; by the light rays of these three letters it is blessed and becomes vast.

[*If done briefly:*]

HA HO HRIH

All faults of color, scent, and potential are purified, and it becomes a great ocean of uncontaminated nectar of exalted wisdom.

OM AH HUM (3x)

Tsok Offering to the Root and Lineage Gurus

HUM

In the blissful skull cup as vast as the three thousand worlds
Is this sacred substance of swirling nectar of tsok offering.
I offer for the sake of delighting the collection of root and lineage
    gurus;
Having accepted, please bless my three doors.

OM AH GURU VAJRADHARA SAPARIWARA GANA CHAKRA
KHAHI PANTSA AMRITA KHAHI

Tsok Offering to Heruka Father and Mother

HUM

In the blissful skull cup as vast as the three thousand worlds
Is this sacred substance of swirling nectar of tsok offering.
I offer for the sake of delighting glorious Heruka Father and Mother;
Having accepted, please bestow the common and supreme attainments.

OM AH SHRI HERUKA VAJRADHARA SAPARIWARA GANA
CHAKRA KHAHI PANTSA AMRITA KHAHI

Tsok Offering to the Four Dakinis

HUM

In the blissful skull cup as vast as the three thousand worlds
Is this sacred substance of swirling nectar of tsok offering.
I offer for the sake of delighting the four dakinis in the directions;
Having accepted, please bestow the common and supreme attainments.

OM AH TSATUR DEWI SAPARIWARA GANA CHAKRA KHAHI
PANTSA AMRITA KHAHI

Tsok Offering to the Collection of Mandala Deities

HUM

In the blissful skull cup as vast as the three thousand worlds
Is this sacred substance of swirling nectar of tsok offering.
I offer for the sake of delighting the collection of mandala deities;
Having accepted, please bestow the common and supreme attainments.

OM AH MANDALA DEWA SAPARIWARA GANA CHAKRA KHAHI
PANTSA AMRITA KHAHI

Tsok Offering to the Three Jewels

HUM

In the blissful skull cup as vast as the three thousand worlds
Is this sacred substance of swirling nectar of tsok offering.
I offer for the sake of delighting the precious and supreme [Three]
    Jewels;
Having accepted, please liberate us from the fears of samsara and peace.

OM AH RATNA TRAYA SAPARIWARA GANA CHAKRA KHAHI
PANTSA AMRITA KHAHI

Tsok Offering to the Dakinis and Dharma Protectors

HUM

In the blissful skull cup as vast as the three thousand worlds
Is this sacred substance of swirling nectar of tsok offering.
I offer for the sake of delighting the collection of dakinis and
    dharma protectors;

Having accepted, please bestow the enlightened actions of yoga.

OM AH DAKINI DHARMAPALA SAPARIWARA GANA CHAKRA KHAHI PANTSA AMRITA KHAHI

Tsok Offering to Mother Sentient Beings

HUM

In the blissful skull cup as vast as the three thousand worlds
Is this sacred substance of swirling nectar of tsok offering.
I offer for the sake of delighting the collection of the six classes of
    mother sentient beings;
Having accepted, please pacify the suffering of mistaken appearance.

OM AH KYATA LU LA ARHA GANA CHAKRA KHAHI PANTSA AMRITA KHAHI

Tsok Offering to the Vajra Master

Then the action vajra offers from his hands some food and drink and says,

Great Hero, please listen to me.
Of this there should be no doubt:
Brahmins, dogs, and outcasts
Are recognized as inseparably one.

Say this, and then the receiver also says,

HUM

I am the principal of all conquerors,
The nature of Bhagawan Heruka Chakrasamvara,
The great ocean of the nectar of exalted wisdom.
I partake to satiate the deities.

AH HO MAHA SUKHA

Say this and partake in the manner of an inner fire offering.

Then bless the leftover tsok offering as done above, and then:

Offering the Leftover Tsok

HUM

In the blissful skull cup as vast as the three thousand worlds
Is this sacred substance of swirling nectar of leftover tsok offering.
I offer for the sake of delighting the collection of oath-bound field
    protectors and so forth;
Having accepted, please establish favorable conditions and remove
    unfavorable conditions.

OM AH KYETRA PALA SAPARIWARA GANA CHAKRA KHAHI
PANTSA AMRITA KHAHI

Say this and send it out.

Colophon

This text was prepared by Dharmabhadra on the moon and day of the
Iron Rabbit Year (1831).[116]

This text was completed on January 17, 2008, the tenth day of the twelfth
month, during the tsok offering day of the special Heruka and Vajrayogini
Month of Gyal Da.

---

116. In "moon and day," "moon" probably refers to Gyal Da—that is, the Heruka and Vajrayogini
month that lasts from the sixteenth day of the eleventh month to the fifteenth day of the twelfth
month. And the "day" probably refers to either the tenth or twenty-fifth day of this same month.

Appendix

SIMPLER DESCRIPTION OF THE CELESTIAL MANSION
IN THE HERUKA FIVE DEITY SADHANA

What follows is a simpler description of the celestial mansion as extracted from the body mandala sadhana composed by Pabongkha Rinpoche. Except for the lotus in the center of the mandala, the two are identical. In the five deity practice the outer edges of the lotus come within one "door-size," or approximately six feet, if you are visualizing yourself as a deity six feet tall. In the body mandala practice, because there are no external deities, the lotus is one half the width of the inside of the celestial mansion.

Furthermore, the celestial mansion is built like a house—square with four doors. The walls are five layers of jewels, colored white, yellow, red, green, and blue, from the outside in. On top of the wall is a red jeweled molding, decorated with triangular, square, and other-shaped jewels. Resting upon this are four layers of golden belts. Through [the top layer] protrude rafters with their ends carved into the shape of sea monsters, with full and half-length pearl necklaces hanging from their mouths. Protruding beyond these are jeweled pendants suspended from the eaves. Above these is a parapet in the shape of half lotus petals. It is adorned with eight victory banners and eight other banners set in golden vases, and the outer four corners are ornamented with parasols.

A red ledge for the objects of desire encircles the outer foot of the wall. Upon this are goddesses of various colors and postures making offerings. At the outer corners of the doorways and hallways, and the four outer and four inner corners of the walls, are half moons upon which abide red jewels adorned at the top by vajras.

At the front of each of the four doors are square pedestals upon which stand four pillars coming from vases; upon these rests an eleven-layered archway. Above each [archway] is a Dharma wheel with a male and female deer to its right and left. To the right and left of each archway, in excellent vases, grow wish-granting trees adorned with the seven precious possessions of a king. All around are siddhas, and emerging from clouds are gods holding garlands of flowers beautifying everything.

Beyond this is a fence of variegated vajras and so forth forming the protection circle. Beyond this, five-colored vajra fires blazing like the fire of destruction at the end of an eon swirl counterclockwise, pervading all directions. Beyond these are the eight charnel grounds with eight trees [one in each charnel ground], with eight directional guardians at their bases. There are eight regional guardians at the tops of the trees with the upper half of their bodies emerging from the branches. There are eight lakes of compassion and eight nagas abiding in them. In the sky above the lakes there are eight clouds. There are eight mountains, upon which rest eight white stupas. There are eight fires of exalted wisdom. Ravens, owls, vultures, wolves, jackals, and bull-headed snakes and so forth move about. Harm-giving spirits, zombies, and cannibals make loud noises such as "kili kili." Mahasiddhas and knowledge-holders who maintain the commitments, as well as yogis and yoginis, all look single-pointedly toward Heruka. They are naked, with loose hair, and are adorned with the five mudras. They hold hand drums, skull cups, and katvangas, and their crowns are adorned with skulls. All who abide in the charnel grounds are laughing and filled with amazement.

Inside the celestial mansion, eight pillars support vajra beams beautifying the roof, which is surmounted at its peak by a precious jeweled vajra. Within the celestial mansion, the ceiling and floor is white in the east, green in the north, red in the west, yellow in the south, and blue in the center. In the center is a lotus of various colors and a sun mandala.

Index

word empowerment, 96

Y
Yamani, 162, 195
Yamantaka, 57
Yanchen Drupay Dorje, 179

Yangchen Drupay Dorje, xi, 115, 157n97
  brief biography of, 7–10
Yongzin Gugay Losang Tenzin, 35

Z
Zongkhar Chöde Monastery, 179, 181

The Dechen Ling Practice Series

Manjushri's Innermost Secret
A Profound Commentary of Oral Instructions on the Practice of Lama Chöpa
Kachen Yeshe Gyaltsen
Foreword by Ganden Tripa Lobsang Tenzin
Now available from Wisdom Publications

The Essence of the Vast and Profound
A Commentary on Je Tsongkhapa's Middle-Length Treatise on the Stages of the Path to Enlightenment
Pabongkha Rinpoche
Now available from Wisdom Publications

The Extremely Secret Dakini of Naropa
Vajrayogini Practice and Commentary
Pabongkha Rinpoche
Now available from Wisdom Publications

The Chakrasamvara Root Tantra
The Speech of Glorious Heruka
Now available from Wisdom Publications

The Roar of Thunder
Yamantaka Practice and Commentary
Ngulchu Dharmabhadra
and the Fifth Ling Rinpoche, Losang Lungtog Tenzin Trinley
Now available from Wisdom Publications

Source of Supreme Bliss
Heruka Chakrasamvara Five Deity Practice
Ngulchu Dharmabhadra,
and the First Panchen Lama, Losang Chökyi Gyaltsen
Now available from Wisdom Publications

Secret Revelations of Chittamani Tara
Generation and Completion Stage Practice and Commentary
Pabongkha Rinpoche

The Blazing Inner Fire of Bliss and Emptiness
An Experiential Commentary on the Practice of the Six Yogas of Naropa
Ngulchu Dharmabhadra

The Melodious Drum of Dakini Land
A Commentary to the Extensive Dedication Prayer of Venerable Vajrayogini
Yangchen Drupay Dorje

Healing Nectar of Immortality
White Tara Healing and Longevity Practices and Commentary
Trijang Rinpoche and Aku Sherab Gyatso

The Ecstatic Dance of Chakrasamvara
Heruka Body Mandala Practice and Commentary
Trijang Rinpoche
Foreword by Gen Lobsang Choephel

About Wisdom Publications

Wisdom Publications is the leading publisher of classic and contemporary Buddhist books and practical works on mindfulness. To learn more about us or to explore our other books, please visit our website at wisdomexperience.org or contact us at the address below.

Wisdom Publications
199 Elm Street
Somerville, MA 02144 USA

We are a 501(c)(3) organization, and donations in support of our mission are tax deductible.

Wisdom Publications is affiliated with the Foundation for the Preservation of the Mahayana Tradition (FPMT).